BOOMING DIGITAL STARS

PRAISE FOR THE BOOK

'Harsh is an outstanding writer! I frequently read his articles and books. The kind of people he covers are truly inspirational, and the insights he shares are beneficial. This book by Harsh and Manish covers the inspiring journeys of individuals who have created their unique paths using digital platforms. Digital is the future! I advise people to learn from these stories and do something innovative and impactful using digital technologies!'

—Anand Kumar, Founder, Super 30

'If the last several decades in marketing were about building sustainable corporate brands, the next decade will be about building personal brands. Harsh Pamnani and Manish Pandey have written a gem on how to build strong personal brands. Everyone who cares about succeeding in a digital world should know and understand the journeys covered in this book.'

—Kartik Hosanagar, John C. Hower Prof. of Technology & Digital Business and Prof. of Marketing, The Wharton School

'Harsh Pamnani and Manish Pandey display a rare intimacy with their subjects. They are candid and objective, yet warm and endearing. Their stories demystify the people we meet in newspaper headlines. They make them human without taking away their glories.'

—Dr Sandeep Goyal, Managing Director, Rediffusion

'Today's digital content creators are change-makers, thought leaders, and bigger than many politicians, cinema and sports stars. 'I would like to congratulate Harsh and Manish for bringing out this revolutionary book with the eleven inspiring journeys of prominent digital content creators of India. This book will not only introduce you to these youth powers, but it will also tell you about India that has become powerful once again. Read on to discover the new India that the world will stand up and salute.'

—Dr Radhakrishnan Pillai, Director, Chanakya International Institute of Leadership Studies and Bestselling Author

'Manish has been tracking TVF literally since the beginning of this creator revolution, when India saw its first-ever original online content in our video *Rowdies* (2012), which became the first viral hit. He had the vision of how this creator economy would explode, more than we as creators did. Given that Manish has guided some of the top creators of India, like BeerBiceps, for over a decade, there is no one better than he, and Harsh, to give us a glimpse of the creators' world.'

—Arunabh Kumar, Pioneer of Web-Series in India and Founder, The Viral Fever (TVF)

BOOMING DIGITAL STARS

11 INSPIRING ADVENTURES FROM INDIA'S CREATOR ECONOMY

HARSH PAMNANI
&
MANISH PANDEY

First published by Pencil Select, an imprint of One Point Six Technologies Pvt. Ltd, in 2021

Published by Westland Business, an imprint of Westland Books, a division of Nasadiya Technologies Private Limited, in 2024

No. 269/2B, First Floor, 'Irai Arul', Vimalraj Street, Nethaji Nagar, Alapakkam Main Road, Maduravoyal, Chennai 600095

ISBN: 9789360459475

10 9 8 7 6 5 4 3 2 1

Typeset by Jojy Philip

Printed at Manipal Technologies Limited, Manipal

We dedicate this book to every creator and every enabler of the emerging creator economy.

And to our families, friends and mentors, who have stood by us always.

Meet the Authors

HARSH PAMNANI

'To create a better version of yourself, surround yourself with the people who are amongst the best in their fields, understand why they are leading and inculcate their good habits. In the digital world, access to a lot of content is both an advantage and a disadvantage. Choose carefully what you consume.'

Harsh is a storyteller by passion and a brand expert by profession. His bestselling book series, *Booming Brands*, was widely acclaimed by eminent academics, Indian government leaders, entrepreneurs and venture capitalists. Harsh also writes for various business publications, including *Forbes.* He has worked with various think tanks like the World Bank, corporates like Deloitte, and start-ups like FirstCry. He also teaches branding at MBA colleges like MICA, Ahmedabad, and business storytelling at IIM Indore. He has spoken at TEDx (seven times), Google Business Group, Josh Talks, IIT Bombay and IIM Ahmedabad. He earned his B.E. in Computer Engineering from IET-DAVV, Indore, and his MBA from XLRI, Jamshedpur.

Contact: www.harshpamnani.com

MANISH PANDEY

'Your past doesn't define your future. If you are honest with yourself and your goal, you can craft an inspiring journey. In the digital world, whoever holds the power of the community is a king or queen of their own space. Sometimes, when people become famous, they show arrogance. Stay humble.'

Manish is a renowned coach and consultant for content creators and start-ups. He also serves as a personal branding advisor to top artists, entrepreneurs and executives. He is the co-founder of BeerBiceps Media, BeerBiceps SkillHouse and BigBrainCo, and the director at BeerBiceps Foundation.

Contact: join2manish@gmail.com
Twitter/Instagram/LinkedIn: @join2manish

CONTENTS

INTRODUCTION

The Twenty-First Century: An Era to Monetise your Creativity

Don't forget: one of the saddest things in life is wasted talent.
—Thomas S. Monson

We are all born with our own innate passions, strengths and talents, such as singing, dancing, acting, cooking, telling stories, making others laugh... But only a few of us are encouraged, either by our parents, or the social system we live in, to turn our passions into professions. *Why is this?*

Perhaps because our elders know of the struggles creative people inevitably face. Every year, many talented people come from India's small towns to large cities like Mumbai, only to face rejection at auditions and interviews. The few who do get a chance to showcase their talent struggle to make a living. Even fewer ever aspire to a comfortable life.

On the other hand, conventional jobs allow people to earn decent livelihoods. Thus, even highly creative people are pushed towards regular jobs with steady salaries. We have all come across people who speak in dull tones about their monotonous jobs but sound excited when describing the stage or debating performances in school or college. Regrettably, they have had to sacrifice their passions to achieve socially acceptable lifestyles.

If this unfortunate reality has been your experience, do not give up just yet, for all is not lost. There is now another scenario.

If you have spent some time on the internet in the last ten years, you will have noticed something different happening in India. From nowhere, digital content companies such as The Viral Fever (TVF) and Pocket Aces have emerged and created national visibility for artists performing at local theatres and gigs. You will also have noticed content creators like Bhuvan Bam, Ashish Chanchlani and Prajakta Koli interviewing film stars and endorsing brands. *Who are they? How did they get here?*

They are regular people who have forged unique paths to success by turning their passions into their professions. Welcome to the new India, where more and more people are making money on the internet by following their passions and doing what they do best. This emerging trend is called the *creator economy*. It is worth our while to explore it in some depth here.

The creator economy features small businesses centered around independent content creators, such as video bloggers, writers, comedians, musicians, etc., who monetise themselves, their skills and their creations. But these small businesses differ from traditional small businesses, such as salons or grocery stores. These new-age small businesses are powered by numerous digital technologies, which give them a global reach from day one. *They go where the internet goes.*

To expand the customer base, a salon manager needs to put in more time and effort. Hence they can only serve a limited number of customers a day, resulting in limited earnings. However, once created, digital assets can be sold infinite times, allowing creators to expand their earnings without expending more time and effort.

Since many people pursue their passions part-time, it is not easy to guess at the figures relating to the creator economy.

However, we found some interesting numbers in the public domain. According to SignalFire,[1] a leading venture capital fund in the creator economy, more than 50 million people worldwide consider themselves creators, despite the creator economy having been born just a decade ago. According to CB Insights,[2] brand deals are the largest monetisation opportunity creators have. But many new monetisation opportunities, such as online courses, subscriptions, their own brands, affiliate links, monetary tips, etc., are also emerging.

You might be curious to know why creators get brand deals. Here is the answer. For a long time, marketers relied on traditional media channels and celebrity endorsements to create brand awareness and boost sales. However, conventional marketing techniques no longer suit the millennials, who prefer social media to watching TV or reading newspapers. Content creators who enjoy a large following on social media are termed influencers. Many influencers forge genuine connections with their followers, who tend to consider them as experts in their respective niches and so take their recommendations seriously. By collaborating with influencers and leveraging their relationship with followers, brands generate awareness and increase sales. This practice is called *influencer marketing*. Generally, the cost of collaboration with a social media influencer is less than collaborating with a film star or cricket celebrity. So, within the same budget, a brand can collaborate with multiple influencers instead of just

---

[1] 'SignalFire's Creator Economy Market Map', *SignalFire*, 29 November 2020, https://www.signalfire.com/blog/creator-economy.

[2] 'The Creator Economy Explained: How Companies Are Transforming The Self-Monetization Boom', *CBInsights*, 15 June 2021, https://www.cbinsights.com/research/report/what-is-the-creator-economy/.

one celebrity, and can achieve tremendous reach with greater frequency. *Now, that makes sense!*

According to a McKinsey article,[3] in 2023, the influencer marketing economy was valued at $21.1 billion. Goldman Sachs estimates that the creator economy could reach $480 billion by 2027.[4] These significant figures suggest that influencers are more likely to impact consumer buying decisions in the immediate future.

You may have already experienced influencer marketing. Recall your interaction with the brand messages of leading start-ups in industries such as fintech, ed-tech, neobank or even fast-moving consumer goods (FMCG), fashion, cosmetics and travel. It is likely you have become aware of many new brands through influencers or friends who follow influencers.

Now let's have a look at some of the technologies and players fuelling the rise of the creator economy.

Creation tools: Steve Jobs once said, 'Technology is nothing. What's important is that you have faith in people, that they're basically good and smart, and if you give them tools, they'll do wonderful things with them.'[5] The tool that laid the foundation of the creator economy was the personal computer. Because of

---

[3] 'What is influencer marketing?', *McKinsey*, 10 April 2023, https://www.mckinsey.com/featured-insights/mckinsey-explainers/what-is-influencer-marketing.

[4] 'The creator economy could approach half-a-trillion dollars by 2027', *Goldman Sachs*, 19 April 2023, https://www.goldmansachs.com/intelligence/pages/the-creator-economy-could-approach-half-a-trillion-dollars-by-2027.html.

[5] Marcel Schwantes, 'Steve Jobs: 'Technology is nothing'—here's what he said it really takes to achieve great success', *CNBC*, 5 October 2019, https://www.cnbc.com/2019/10/05/apple-ceo-steve-jobs-technology-is-nothing-heres-what-it-takes-to-achieve-great-success.html.

computers, people began to create information digitally. When information became digital, it became easier to edit, share and search. Another tool that has accelerated the growth of this economy is the user-friendly smartphone with its powerful digital camera. Smartphones allow even amateurs to become professional photographers and videographers. Numerous tools have emerged to help creators express their creativity. For instance, many artists use GarageBand to create music. Design tools like Canva allow creators to create visual content. The online recording platform Riverside.fm enables creators to record studio-quality videos and podcasts.

With the advent of AI tools, the productivity of creators has significantly increased. They are utilising AI-driven tools to explore trending topics, understand audience preferences, refine their creative concepts and automate repetitive tasks. This shift is not only increasing their productivity but also ensuring that creators can meet the increasing demand for diverse and engaging content in today's digital era. As AI technology continues to advance, there will be a more seamless integration of AI into every facet of content creation.

Media platforms: For decades, large media houses controlled the world of content. Editors held the power to make or break the destiny of any struggling artist. Now internet-enabled platforms have changed the game by removing the traditional gatekeepers. These platforms help creators distribute their creations, get discovered and establish an audience base. For example, the blogging platform Medium is popular with writers, the audio streaming platform Spotify with musicians and podcasters, and the online video-sharing platform YouTube with video-bloggers and film-makers. By creating visibility through these platforms, creators can earn the social currency of reputation and attention, which can then be monetised in various ways. Many platforms also split their ad revenue with creators.

You might wonder how good and bad creators are differentiated on these platforms. The quick answer is that these platforms capture audience feedback in the form of comments, likes and shares. This online word of mouth acts as a catalyst to connect to new audiences, *like a chain of reinforcement*. These platforms have algorithms that help in recommending suitable content to different audiences.

Creator management agencies: Once creators have built a substantial audience base, they are approached by brands to advertise products and services. Events, performances and speaking opportunities emerge. To remain trusted with their audience base, creators have to be careful about the brands they choose to partner with. They cannot sacrifice content quality to push a brand message. These commercial transactions can divert a creator's focus from their primary activity—creating exciting content for their specific audience.

This is where the role of talent management agencies comes in. They alleviate the commercial pressure on creators by selecting brand deals, negotiating contracts, planning brand campaigns and conducting in-depth post-campaign analysis. For their service, these agencies take a percentage of the creator's earnings. In the past few years, many talent management agencies have emerged in India, of which Monk Entertainment (Monk-E), Artist Aadmi, Opraahfx and One Digital Entertainment are the best-known.

Creator marketplaces: Marketplaces act as intermediaries between creator supply and customer demand. To use an analogy, these marketplaces are like Uber and Amazon, where creators can sign up and start earning revenue with a minimal set-up. Marketplaces typically charge creators a subscription fee, plus a percentage on brand campaigns. These marketplaces have built-in analytics and reporting capabilities that help brands analyse their campaign outcomes. To name a few examples, Gumroad enables creators to sell software, e-books, PDFs and other digital goods. TagMango and Pepper Content are the leading marketplaces of Indian origin that have empowered creators to become financially independent. Marketplaces flourish when they provide sufficient growth opportunities to creators. So, besides customers, marketplaces provide necessary tools and training to creators. For instance, Teachable's online teacher community provides a dedicated space for creators in a similar business phase to network.

Creator-focused studios: New-age studios are being launched to provide content creators with the tools and space they need to excel. They are not just about the space, but about an entire ecosystem designed to make content creation efficient, cost-effective and creatively inspiring. Creators can choose between three plug-and-play sets to experiment with different aesthetics and scenarios. These studios also curate a roster of professionals, including stylists, photographers, videographers and editors, whom creators can handpick based on their project requirements. Unlike traditional shooting spaces, everyone involved—camerapersons, editors, set designers and more—has a digital-first approach. They understand the required formats and versatility in editing and shooting, and they effectively incorporate the latest technology.

As more creators enter the supply side, more ecosystem players, tools and business models are emerging to support them. For instance, in 2022, Instagram launched a creator marketplace that allows brands to find creators they may want to connect with. Interestingly, venture capital funding in the creator economy start-up space has skyrocketed. Many global as well as Indian start-ups have raised millions of dollars from marquee investors. Some investors are also coming forward to invest in individual creators.

You will have realised by reading thus far that the creator economy is BOOMING! The market will inevitably see a crowding of creators. When a market gets crowded, the customer (demand) gets numerous choices, while the creator (supply) faces immense competition. But a plethora of choices also leads to customer confusion. A wrong choice can spoil their experience and turn them away. As a case in point, if multiple customers experience poor-quality work, this emerging economy could collapse.

To avoid confusion and get desired value, customers use brands as quality-guarantee shortcuts to make choices. In fact, they pay a higher price for a trustworthy brand even if an unknown alternative is available at a lower price. As in the products market, brands are also preferred in the creator market. However, many creators are clueless about what they need to do to stand out as a brand. There are also popular misconceptions. Many creators think that by gaining social media followers, they can create their brand. That is incorrect. A personal brand is not made just by the number of social media followers. Customers do not look for general popularity but rather seek out a creator who is *known for something*. In marketing terms, what they look for is a *brand with positioning*.

You know by now that though the size of the creator economy is humongous and the available opportunities immense, the chances of creators getting lost in the crowd are higher than the chances of getting noticed. But where there are problems, there is also literature with case studies and solutions. There have been many books written about becoming the CEO of a large corporation or creating a fast-growing start-up, and business schools teach how to analyse and manage large businesses. But it is hard to find a book or business school course on creating and managing *a single-person brand in an emerging creator economy*. Hence this book. You may justifiably wonder what special insights we have to offer. Read on and you will find details of the solutions we have created.

Though the market is crowded, India has seen the rise of an entirely new breed of first-generation creators who have established powerful personal brands through their content, entrepreneurial mindset and social media. Due to their increasing popularity and credibility, they are often perceived as role models, not just by their followers, but businesses, mainstream media and Bollywood (in itself a great influencer). These creators have begun replacing or working along with traditional celebrities, such as film stars and athletes in brand endorsements and promotions. They are even seen in web series and movies. In this book, you will find eleven stories of leading Indian creators and gain insights on:

1. How they started from scratch;
2. How they achieved popularity in a highly crowded and competitive market;
3. How they identify new ideas for content creation and brand collaboration.

And much more. The lessons captured in these stories will help aspiring and emerging creators build their brand in their chosen niche. If you have a skill, you have an opportunity to shine a light on it and earn a livelihood. Why sit and wait for Godot when you can leverage the power of the creator economy? Move ahead to turn your passion into your profession.

We wish you a great innings in the marketplace.

Before you tell yourself, you have no right to invent this or improve that, remind yourself that the person before you had no right either, but did it anyway.

—Seth Godin

BHUVAN BAM

BHUVAN BAM

From Restaurant Singer to High-Value Digital Star

'Work hard in silence; let your success be your noise.'
—Frank Ocean

When you think of Indian cinema, which name comes to mind first? Amitabh Bachchan, perhaps? He is generally regarded as one of the greatest and most influential actors in the history of Indian cinema. And when you think of the Indian start-up ecosystem, which name comes to mind? Flipkart, maybe? It is generally thought to be India's biggest and most successful start-up story. And when you consider Indian YouTubers, which name springs to mind? Certainly Bhuvan Bam's, acknowledged as one of India's greatest YouTube sensations.

Bhuvan was the first Indian to hit 2 million subscribers on YouTube. As impressive as that is, he was also the first Indian to cross 10 million subscribers on YouTube. As of April 2024, over 56 million people follow him on various social media channels. Bhuvan's life is a classic rags-to-riches story. A youngster of eighteen, he would sing gigs at Delhi's Moti Mahal Deluxe restaurant, for a meagre monthly earning of ₹3,000. While his pockets were practically empty, he was full of hope and aspiration.

By the age of twenty-five, he was a self-made millionaire.

The winner of dozens of awards such as Global Entertainer of the Year, at the World Bloggers Awards in Cannes, France, Most Popular Channel on YouTube, at the WebTVAsia Awards held in South Korea, Bhuvan also appeared on *Forbes India*'s 30 Under 30 list. He was the first Indian YouTuber to attend the annual meeting of the World Economic Forum at Davos, Switzerland.

Bhuvan's achievements did not end there. He appeared in the short film, *Plus Minus*, which earned him a Filmfare Award. In December 2018, he began a digital series on YouTube called *Titu Talks*, that featured Shah Rukh Khan as his first guest. By February 2021, he had released seven music videos, including *Heer Ranjha*, which became the #1 hit song across charts on iTunes within an hour of its release. Bhuvan is one of the few influencers in India associated with multiple famous brands, including Myntra, The Man Company, Tissot, Pizza Hut and Lenskart. Bhuvan also started one of India's first creator-led merchandise brands, Youthiapa, and a production company, BB Ki Vines Productions, which has produced *Dhindora*, the first Indian web series to cross half a billion views and *Taaza Khabar*, one of the most-watched Indian web series in 2023, and several other shows. He also served as the Hindi-language commentator for the 2023 reboot of the Japanese game show *Takeshi's Castle*.

But success was not instantaneous. When Bhuvan started his YouTube journey, his first four videos received only fifteen views. However, in less than five years, Bhuvan had become India's first digital content creator with 3 billion collective views. Considering his humble beginnings, Bhuvan's journey is the stuff we dream of. But it is true.

This is his story.

THE BEGINNING

Bhuvan Bam was born on 22 January 1994, in Baroda, Gujarat, into a middle-class family. His family later moved to Delhi. As a child, Bhuvan had little interest in academics. He preferred to watch movies featuring the noted comedians of Hindi cinema—Govinda, Kader Khan, Johnny Lever... Repeating their filmi dialogues became a favourite pastime. His passion and natural flair for comedy was not limited to the home. In school, he would entertain his fellow pupils by mimicking their teachers. Besides comedy, he loved sketching. While others bent to their books in class, he would doodle and draw.

When Bhuvan was in Class IV, his mother enrolled him in a classical music class. Initially, he found it very dull. But as he gradually grew to understand that classical music was the foundation of all types of music, he applied himself seriously. He learnt to play the harmonium, keyboard and guitar. Music became an instrinsic part of his life.

Bhuvan's goal was to be a singer–musician. However, his parents, especially his mother, wanted him to get a B. Com degree from the prestigious Delhi University (DU). The cut-off for the B. Com course in the top colleges ranged between 91 per cent and 99 per cent. In Junior College, Bhuvan scored 74 per cent, far below the required percentile for admission. He ended up choosing to study history at Shaheed Bhagat Singh College, DU.

During his undergraduate years, Bhuvan joined a Delhi-based band called Astitva. The band performed gigs at restaurants and private parties. In early 2015, a turning point arrived when he saw a news video covering the floods in Kashmir. In the video, a journalist asked a mother who had just lost her child in the floods how she felt. Bhuvan was stunned by the insensitivity shown by the reporter. Using his newly brought smartphone, he did a 15-second satire on the reporter and put it up on Facebook.

The video got fifteen views and a few likes. Unfazed, Bhuvan posted three more videos on his profile page. One of his friends told him these dramatic videos did not look good on his profile page and it would be better if Bhuvan created a separate Facebook page and did his experiments there. At the time, Vine was a very popular video hosting service that allowed people to post and share 6-second video shorts. As Bhuvan's videos were also short, he thought he would create a Facebook page under the name BB Ki Vines (Bhuvan Bam Ki Vines).

Since his school days, Bhuvan has loved making people laugh, cracking jokes and doing mimicry. So, he decided to post his comedy videos on his newly created Facebook page. The first video with double entendre was titled 'I am Feeling Horny'. It first became popular among his college friends. From college WhatsApp groups, the video travelled to other colleges, and suddenly he was famous as far afield as Karachi University! Soon the video crossed 15,000 views, and within a week, Bhuvan had over 30,000 fans on Facebook.

As he posted more videos, his fame spread, and within eight months, he had over 800,000 followers on Facebook. Seeing the response to his videos, a friend suggested Bhuvan shift to YouTube, as he could earn from the videos as well. In late 2015, Bhuvan started his YouTube channel.

There are many valuable lessons to be learnt from the evolution of Bhuvan Bam as a personal brand. Here are some of them.

HUSTLE AND ITERATE TO FIND YOUR RIGHT MARKET

Marketing guru Seth Godin once said, 'Everyone is not your customer.' Finding a market with customers who welcome you with open arms does not happen immediately. In the background, many iterations happen with the product (creator), and trials and rejections take place in different markets. But once the right fit between product and market is found, growth picks up.

To validate this point, here is a true story. In the 1960s, a tall and thin young man did a voice audition at All India Radio, but was rejected. He wanted to be an actor, but many film-makers rejected him because of his height and unconventional looks. He did a few minor roles in small films, none of which took his acting career anywhere. By the age of thirty, he had twelve flops to his name. But he refused to give up, continuously working to improve his craft.

In the 1970s, the romantic hero dominanted Bollywood, and many of the popular lead actors of the day turned down the 'angry young man' role in an action film called *Zanjeer*. It was finally offered to our struggling young actor. Perhaps it was a fortunate alignment of stars. Audiences were looking for a change from stereotypical romances to action-oriented films. *Zanjeer* became a super-hit and turned our struggling actor into a well-known star—Amitabh Bachchan. And as they say, the rest is history.

In a similar vein, the start of Bhuvan's journey had been nothing short of a bumpy ride. He had failed to get into a B. Com course at every college he applied to and was compelled to shift academic focus to History. During the two-month vacation before college began, he thought he would work and earn some pocket money. Randomly, he applied for a delivery boy job at a Domino's outlet in the Malviya Nagar area of Delhi. There too, he was rejected.

Bhuvan had been learning music from a musician named Salman Khan, who performed at Moti Mahal Deluxe Restaurant in Delhi's Saket area. One night, Salman's brother was not available to play the guitar, so he asked Bhuvan to accompany him. The incentive was a free dinner. Bhuvan readily agreed. That day, Bhuvan learnt that he could make money by playing music at the restaurant. For the next two years, he performed every day, Monday to Sunday, from 8 p.m. till midnight, receiving ₹3,000 as a monthly salary and free food. Encouraged by the appreciation the patrons displayed for his music, Bhuvan began writing his own songs and composing his own music. He had become what he had always wanted to be—a popular singer-musician.

To gain recognition as a musician, he applied to almost every reality show in India. He stood in line for hours before being rejected or shown the door without an audition. On one such occasion, Bhuvan waited for an audition from 6 a.m. to 2 p.m. Then he was told the audition would happen the next day, based on token numbers. The person then threw tokens into the air. To catch the tokens, candidates were jumping on each other. Seeing this pathetic treatment of artists, Bhuvan hit his nadir. He decided then that he would never again attend a reality show audition.

When he heard about an opportunity with Fox Star Studios, he prepared and shared seven songs with the selection team. He was rejected, and received nothing for his efforts. Trying his hand at comedy, Bhuvan sent numerous mails to OTT platforms. None of his emails were answered. He also participated in several comedy hunt competitions, but was never recognised for his performance.

But Bhuvan was not ready to give up. Despite the many rejections, he kept honing his skills and pitching to different platforms. Eventually, he found YouTube as a medium to showcase his talent in comedy, singing and acting. Incredibly, he garnered 1 million subscribers on YouTube within seven months. Due to his rising popularity, in 2016, Bhuvan earned a collaboration opportunity with The Viral Fever (TVF), one of the leading OTT platforms in India. Today, Bhuvan is considered the poster boy of YouTube stardom in India. 'Rejections can break you, but they certainly make you,' he says.

DARE TO DIFFERENTIATE YOURSELF

One of the core principles of brand building is differentiation. Marketing Guru Al Ries said, 'A branding program should be designed to differentiate your cow from all the other cattle on the range. Even if all the cattle on the range look pretty much alike.' So how did Bhuvan differentiate himself in the crowded comedy space?

People want a break from their stressed lives, and comedy is a great way to do that. Perhaps that's why numerous stand-up comedy acts are performed in every big city, and there are countless comedy videos on YouTube. Comedy is big business in India and hence a crowded category. Every day, it becomes more difficult for a comedian to stand out. Moreover, your jokes can be copied, and there is no guarantee that you will please everyone. In such a tough market, the rise of Bhuvan Bam is truly commendable.

At the very start, Bhuvan realised that if he wanted to take up comedy for any length of time, he would have to do things differently. He noticed that online content consumption was mainly in English, by an English-speaking audience. To differentiate himself, he chose street humour in Hindi, with a heavy dosage of Delhi slang. He also found that comedy videos were filled with insults to others. Again, to differentiate his act, Bhuvan chose to write scripts that had some meaningful message, delivered in a funny way. Initially, he aimed at college-going, middle-class youth. But later, he started creating funny content around the problems faced by every middle-class household in India.

Another challenge in comedy is to remain fresh and come up with different content each time. To develop a style and tone that made him different from the others in the space, Bhuvan created nineteen quirky characters, portrayed by himself. This kind of character-based comedy by a single performer had not been done in India before. He started off these characters with parents, then added three best friends, and then Titu Mama, modelled on his own uncle, followed by others. These characters were full of life and true to their personifications. People could identify them in their daily lives.

Bhuvan says, 'To make a good joke, you need a good concept and a great script.' To find concepts, Bhuvan observes people and situations carefully. He says the Delhi metro is a great place to observe people and pick up traits for characters. He spends a lot of time going in-depth into a concept and spends about two weeks preparing a script. He picks a clichéd storyline and then builds a strong plot with his lively characters. He also incorporates crisp punchlines and timely dialogue. Then he spends 4–5 hours creating the video.

Unlike the videos of many other artists, Bhuvan develops his at zero production cost. He shoots with his phone camera, without a tripod, which means he has only one free hand to act. 'I can hold the camera without a selfie stick for 20 minutes at a stretch,' he likes to tell people. Moreover, instead of shooting his videos at fancy locations, he shoots them in a small room in a middle-class home. On digital platforms, people prefer crisp content. Therefore, after a shoot, Bhuvan spends 15–20 hours editing his 4- or 5-hour video to turn it into 4–5 minutes. The simplicity and relatability of his content have made him vastly popular.

Hiding emotion and feeling is another tricky part of being a comedian. A comedian has to make people laugh irrespective of what he might be feeling. As a case in point, Bhuvan's elder brother Aman was in a major road accident just after receiving his pilot's license. He survived but was laid up at home for over six years. His dream of becoming a pilot had slipped from his hand. Often, while making his audience laugh, Bhuvan's personal life was full of tears for his brother. During those trying years, Bhuvan never stopped motivating his brother to look at a better future.

Cut from the same cloth as his brother, Aman did not give up. Today, he is a pilot with Indigo Airlines. Bhuvan says, 'The day Aman achieved his dream, the four of us (my parents, my brother and I), celebrated with a pizza party at home. It was the best night!'

PARTNER WITH PEOPLE WHO SEE YOUR VALUE

Artists create the best output when they enjoy their work. But to support themselves, they also need to earn. When they try to do both, one or the other aspect gets impacted. Greg Norman, a successful athlete turned businessmen, believed, 'Our success is a direct result of knowing how to market a brand and having the right people representing the brand.' Collaboration between an artist and a business partner who represents the artist can create enormous value. That is exactly what happened when Bhuvan found his business partner and manager, Rohit Raj.

Brought up in a business family, entrepreneurship came naturally to Rohit. While a student at Delhi Public School,

Greater Noida, he was the president of co-curricular activities. He would organise interschool, inter-DPS and inter-district competitions, with a footfall of 500–20,000. Encouraged by the success and appreciation he garnered for his work, he wished to become an event organiser. His father however, wished him to pursue engineering. Rohit did start at an engineering college in Shimla, but he did not enjoy the subjects and failed the first-year exams. Depressed, Rohit locked himself in his hostel room for a week. He stopped eating and talking to friends. He was ashamed to face his parents, thinking he had wasted their money and broken their dreams. To his astonishment, when he finally reached home, his father merely asked, 'What do you want to do?' Rohit was unsure what he would do, but he was sure it would not be engineering.

Three months later, Rohit started his events company, Rohit Raj Events. He was desperate to prove himself. Having made hundreds of calls, he finally got the chance to organise a college festival for a prominent university in Meerut. At the age of nineteen, he found himself dealing with numerous vendors, artists and teachers, none of whom took him seriously. But Rohit was determined not to fail again. He would tell people, 'I am just nineteen years old, but I am here to give my best. I will not let you down.'

The event was a success, and it gave Rohit a sense of accomplishment. Rohit says, 'The feeling was good, but it became even better when I gave my first pay cheque to my mother. She was proud and her trust in me was a good feeling.' In another year, by the age of twenty, Rohit was working with Indian rap artists like Badshah and Raftaar. By the time he was twenty-five, Rohit had done over a hundred shows. By February 2021, he was running five ventures, including BB Ki Vines Production and Youthiapa, with Bhuvan.

Bhuvan and Rohit struggled on separate paths till destiny brought them together one day. Rohit was organising a college event, and the students insisted he invite Bhuvan Bam. Rohit had never heard of him, so he searched the internet and discovered Bhuvan's funny videos. Rohit invited Bhuvan to the event. The two young men connected on topics as varied as creativity, struggle, fears and dreams. For the next six months, they travelled together to multiple events and found magical chemistry. Eventually, Rohit became Bhuvan's manager.

The coming together of Bhuvan's art and Rohit's business sense was a magical combination. In no time, they had created and delivered several masterpieces. Rohit produced Bhuvan's trending songs like *Safar*, *Sang Hoon Tere*, *Rahguzar*, *Bas Mein*, *Ajnabee*, *Heer Ranjha* and the mini-series *Dhindora*. In 2018, Rohit produced Bhuvan's short film *Plus Minus*, which won the 2019 Filmfare Award for Best Short Film.

Rohit also takes care of Bhuvan's brand associations, live shows and media engagements. The duo has been very selective in their engagements. Of ten brands, they perhaps pick the two that genuinely resonate with Bhuvan and his audience. They only enter into partnerships if Bhuvan is happy to use the brand himself. 'Our focus is to ensure Bhuvan doesn't come across as hard-selling products,' explains Rohit. 'Brand integration in Bhuvan's content happens organically, like using Lenskart glasses for his characters or wearing a Tissot watch. This doesn't look like hard-selling, but the brand reaches our audience,' says Rohit.

The duo also launched BB Ki Vines merchandise, such as t-shirts, coffee mugs and phone cases, with Bhuvan dialogues and character sketches. These products are sold through Youthiapa.

Bhuvan and Rohit have witnessed many ups and downs together. Bhuvan says, 'Rohit has been a constant support since the day we met. Now, we have worked together so much that our individual dreams have merged to become common dreams.' The bond and respect they share is as inspiring as it is unusual. Bhuvan says it best, 'We are more than brothers.'

DON'T LOSE YOUR FOCUS BECAUSE OF OTHERS' OPINIONS

Focus is essential to building a brand. However, many lose their focus by listening to naysayers. Steve Jobs said, 'Your time is limited, so don't waste it living someone else's life. Don't be trapped by dogma, which is living with the results of other people's thinking. Don't let the noise of others' opinions drown out your own inner voice. And most important, have the courage to follow your heart and intuition.' Bhuvan's journey is a testament to these words.

An unconventional career is looked at with suspicion in traditional Indian society. Parents are usually skeptical and worried when their children choose not to go down the tried and tested paths, such as a government job, engineer, doctor, CA, etc. The same happened with Bhuvan. His mother, Padma Bam, worked in a private company, while his father, Avnindra Bam, was a retired government employee. They wanted Bhuvan to prepare for the bank exam. But Bhuvan was not interested in academics or doing a conventional job. He never had been.

When Bhuvan began singing at a restaurant and at private parties, while in college, his parents hated it and opposed it vehemently. But for Bhuvan, it was an opportunity to gain exposure and shed stage fright. In the two years he sang at the restaurant, he did not take a single day's leave. When his parents saw his commitment to his choice, they stopped arguing with him. The day Bhuvan got his first cheque of ₹20,000 from

YouTube, he went to the restaurant owner and expressed his desire to leave. The team at the restaurant were sad to see him go but knew they could not tie down a flying eagle.

When he started creating videos full time, Bhuvan's parents had no idea what he was doing all day in his room. They were worried their son would not listen to them, concerned about what he would do with his life. In one of his videos, Bhuvan made fun of a condom. The condom brand used in the video noticed Bhuvan and offered him a brand endorsement. As this was his first brand deal, Bhuvan excitedly shared the news with his mother, telling her that brands have begun to approach him for endorsements. Less excited, Padma Bam asked, 'Which brand has approached you?' Bhuvan gathered his courage and told her it was a condom brand. She was shocked. Bhuvan tried to convince her that he would just be creating a comedy video, nothing else. But his mother was unhappy.

The next day, without informing Bhuvan, the brand sent a box of condoms to his home. Bhuvan was not in and it was father, Avnindra Bam, who opened the box. As shocked as his wife had been, he immediately called Bhuvan. 'You are moving on the wrong path!' he told his son. When Bhuvan reached home, he was not sure how his father would react. Surprisingly, Avnindra Bam told him, 'We have always been proud of you. I hope you will not let us down.' Then he asked his son to get ready for dinner.

One evening, Bhuvan's parents suggested he join them for Diwali shopping at Sarojini Nagar Market, in New Delhi. Because of his rising popularity, Bhuvan was wary of being seen at such a public place. He told his father, 'A few days ago, a crowd of youngsters gathered around me at IFFCO Chowk Metro Station. They wanted to share their appreciation for my work, but the situation caused inconvenience to other people.

I don't want to create any inconvenience for you and others in the market.'

Bhuvan's father thought Bhuvan was joking and took him along anyway. As Bhuvan had anticipated, a crowd of youngsters gathered around him. Finally, policemen came to manage the situation. They took Bhuvan to a corner and asked him questions like: Who are you? What have you done? Why is there such a crowd? When Bhuvan told them that he was a YouTuber and all the youngsters were his fans, the policemen looked astonished and then quickly took a picture with him. He had to request them to help him find his parents as they were not visible in the crowd.

Eventually, the family returned, without any shopping. On the way back, Avnindra Bam said to his son, 'Maybe you are doing something that we don't understand, but these youngsters understand. Next time you join us, please wear a mask.' Thereafter, gradually, his father started giving Bhuvan feedback on his videos and even suggesting a few ideas for interesting storylines.

One day, a relative called Avnindra Bam to share the news that his son had got a job. He also asked about Bhuvan's career plans. Bhuvan's father congratulated the relative on his son's good fortune, then said, 'Bhuvan has 10 million followers on YouTube. I am confident he will do something amazing!'

Along with love, Bhuvan also receives criticism from his audience. Sometimes, people criticise him for not posting content, and sometimes they criticise him for not posting good content. When he began, abusive comments and messages would affect Bhuvan. But something his father said changed his perspective: 'When you are rising, there will always be people behind you. Some will try to pull you down, and some will push you to rise up. You can't please everyone. Rather than trying to satisfy haters, you should dedicate your time to people who actually adore and respect your work.' With time, Bhuvan learnt to differentiate between criticism and hate. A genuine critic asks you to improve your content. In contrast, a hater always abuses you, no matter what. Bhuvan takes criticism constructively and makes enormous effort to improve every area of his offering. He ignores hate.

Bhuvan did not take long to prove himself. Within a few years, he had gifted a luxurious apartment to his parents. Everyone at home was happy. But then disaster struck. Avnindra Bam had a stroke. Following brain surgery, he lost much of his memory. Earlier, when Bhuvan would reach home, his father would say, '*Mera beta aa gaya*,' (my son has come) but now he just looked at Bhuvan, with no reaction. During this challenging period, *Kaun Banega Crorepati* (KBC) acted as a catalyst of hope for the family. Avnindra Bam watched the show eagerly. In a heartwarming tweet, Bhuvan thanked Amitabh Bachchan and the makers of the show.

BRANDS WITH HUMILITY TOUCH HEARTS

Seth Godin says, 'Brand humility is the only response to a fast-changing and competitive marketplace. The humble brand understands that it needs to re-earn attention, re-earn loyalty and reconnect with its audience, as if every day is the first day.' Humility has been instrumental in Bhuvan's rise too, in an increasingly crowded and competitive digital space. Though he has delivered many #1 trending YouTube videos, Bhuvan still feels he is just beginning. He feels that achieving something is not a big thing, but sustaining it is an art. Not many people can. 'I always remember where I came from and whatever I am today is because of my audience,' he says.

With fans and a larger audience base comes the pressure to create more thoughtful content. Bhuvan keeps noting down ideas as they come to him and analyses what is working and what isn't. He says, 'Initially, I was making content for fun. But now, I do feel a certain sense of responsibility towards my viewers.' Sometimes, the pressure of being constantly funny and creative gets to Bhuvan. Sometimes, he experiences creative block. Perhaps that is why he is consciously working on fewer videos now and continually raising the quality of content.

Bhuvan firmly believes that if a creator assumes that by achieving some fame, they have become a star then they are on the wrong path. He suggests that when a creator is interacting with fans, followers and admirers, they should put ego aside. 'I always remember that my followers have many other options. By watching my videos, they are doing me a favour. I value their affection a lot.' After posting anything on social media, Bhuvan interacts with his audience for at least 30 minutes. Every fortnight, he tries to go live on Instagram from midnight to 3 a.m. On Instagram, he does not discuss BB Ki Vines; instead, he interacts with his audience and does live music sessions. As Instagram live sessions last an hour each, after 56 minutes, he asks his audience whether he should come back. By the time he is done with his three sessions, his phone is extremely hot.

Sometimes, people share their frustrations with him. They say things like, 'I am not getting anywhere. I have lost hope. I don't know what to do.' That's something he finds challenging to respond to as the path to earning from one's passion is not straightforward. Bhuvan feels that content creators have to keep making content because only then will they learn. If someone expects overnight success, they have entered the field with the wrong mindset. It takes a lot of hard work, determination and consistency to achieve success. One has to be patient and keep hustling.

When Bhuvan began his journey, he had not expected even 1,000 followers. But with patience and perseverance, he has achieved many milestones. He now says, '*Aaj bhi, mera junoon same hain. But maturity jayada hain. I still have a long way to go.*' ('Even today, my passion is the same. But I am more mature.') Bhuvan has plans to release more music videos, and he wants to establish himself as a songwriter in Bollywood. But all this is not enough for him. *Ye Dil maange more.* And so, he speaks enthusiastically about his desire to make a separate movie with each of his characters, and develop BB Universe into another Marvel Comic Universe.

It will be fascinating to see how the brand Bhuvan Bam evolves in the years to come.

IN CONCLUSION

There was a time when pursuing a career in media and entertainment required good looks, art or film school degrees, or parental pedigree. One was required to stand in queues for hours just to audition. But social media has changed the world. Now, anyone can showcase their talent on YouTube. Bhuvan Bam's fantastic journey from restaurant singer to high-value digital star is an excellent example of the power of social media.

The word 'unicorn' is often used to describe something desirable and elusive. Creators like Bhuvan Bam are extremely rare. Undoubtedly, he is a unicorn in the world of content creators.

Perspectives from Bhuvan Bam

- Choose your friends wisely. Surround yourself with the right set of people, who will be truthful and give you a clear picture of life.
- There is a thin line between confidence and overconfidence. If you cross this line by mistake, you can get into trouble. Self-doubt is a boon. When you have self-doubt, you make extra effort and behave more tactfully.
- When you are in a state of self-doubt, do not talk to too many people. Only to those you can really trust to be your sounding board.
- Do not pin all your hopes on something. When things do not work out, we start cribbing. Stop having great expectations. Do not chase things. Focus on doing good work. Good things will come to you automatically.
- If you have a plan or an idea, do not share it with everyone. You never know who will use your idea without your knowledge. If you genuinely want to grow in life, keep your plans secret. If required, discuss them only with select people.
- If you want to do something different in life, then do it. But make sure you don't ignore studies. Education is important.
- Very few people get a chance to do what they love. If you are getting a chance to do something you like, don't hesitate to give more than 100 per cent.

ASHISH CHANCHLANI

ASHISH CHANCHLANI

From Aspiring Actor to One of India's Best-Loved Content Creators

Young man, make your name worth something.

—Andrew Carnegie

When you are born with a silver spoon in your mouth, people expect you to have a comfortable life, flaunt family wealth and live the high life with parties and luxuries. It is most unlikely that such a person would choose the road less taken and make a name for himself. But so it was with Ashish Chanchlani, who preferred to disregard inherited comforts to earn his claim to fame by carving a niche through hard work, grit and determination.

Ashish is the scion of an affluent Sindhi business family. However, instead of joining the established family business, he chose a different path. When he started his journey, digital content was not the popular space in India that it is today. His extended family would tell his parents that by wasting time on digital platforms, Ashish was making the biggest mistake of his life. But instead of listening to others, Ashish preferred to follow the beat of a different drum.

Today, Ashish is regarded as one of India's biggest digital entertainers. As of April 2024, over 60 million people follow him on YouTube, Facebook, X (formerly Twitter) and Instagram. He has collaborated with Bollywood stars like Akshay Kumar, Shahid Kapoor, Kartik Aaryan, Rajkumar Rao and rapper Badshah. He has been associated with Marvel Studios for *Avengers: Infinity War* and *Avengers: Endgame*. He also did a cameo in *Men In Black: International*.

His long list of awards provides audience validation for his work. In 2018, Ashish was awarded the Dadasaheb Phalke International Film Festival Award for Best Digital Influencer. In 2019, he won the Best Comedy Influencer at the first edition of World Bloggers Awards held at the Cannes Film Festival. In 2020, he won Favourite YouTuber at Nickelodeon Kids' Choice Awards, India. In 2021, he was included in *Forbes India*'s 30 Under 30 list. In 2022, he was listed in *Forbes India*'s list of Top 100 Digital Stars.

Ashish has attained far greater success than anyone would have dared to suggest when he began. This is his story—of creating a brand identity using his individuality as the main tool.

THE BEGINNING

Ashish was born on 8 December 1993, in Ulhasnagar, a suburb of Mumbai. From childhood, Ashish displayed a mad love for movies, enhanced by the fact that his family has been in the cinema hall business. So, he was at liberty to study acting by sitting in a theatre, watching movies.

Ever since he could remember, Ashish wanted to use his acting skills to entertain people. But he never got an opportunity to perform on stage. The reason was that his teachers always picked the smart and good-looking kids to perform. Ashish was both chubby and shy. When he was in Class VIII, his Social Studies teacher caught him mimicking his PT teacher. Ashish was given a warning. However, impressed by Ashish, the teacher offered him the role of a news reporter in a school play. Sadly, Ashish could not relate to the role and disappointed his audience.

A few months later, another play was to be performed at the school's annual day function. During a rehearsal, the student playing the funny Trash King's role was absent, and Ashish called in as his temporary replacement. Instead of following the script, Ashish added his own comic flavour to the role, and everybody loved his act. As a result, the absent student was replaced. Ashish performed well and won hearts. From that day on, Ashish was a regular in school dramas.

When he finished school, Ashish expressed his desire to become an actor. Being associated with the film industry, his father understood the challenges of such a career all too well. He told Ashish, 'If you want to become an actor, I won't be stopping you, but this road is long, and it is full of struggles. It is full of obstacles. It can disappoint you. It can break you.' Not knowing how to react to these blunt truths, Ashish's acting dream died in that moment. Since he was academically bright and had done well in his final board examinations, numerous voices suggested pursue science. He chose civil engineering and entered Datta Meghe College of Engineering, Navi Mumbai.

Ashish did not enjoy his engineering subjects and often thought of leaving and moving to his first love—acting. But his father advised him that one should always have an education, no matter what field one was interested in. So, Ashish continued with his engineering studies. Simultaneously, he started creating short funny videos on the social media app, Vine. From 6-second Vine videos, Ashish moved to making 15-second Instagram videos. He discovered that someone had posted a compilation of his Instagram videos on YouTube. He also got to know that YouTube pays creators when they reach a certain level of viewership. This excited him and he began exploring possibilities.

In December 2014, Ashish made his first YouTube video, 'How to annoy people who say *Tu Mere Baap Ko Janta Nahi Hai*' ('you don't know who my father is', in colloquial Hindi). The video went viral. At the time, his dream was to have 100,000 subscribers and earn the YouTube Silver Play Button. No one, least of all himself, ever imagined that he would become one of the most popular YouTubers in India, with millions of followers.

There are many valuable lessons to be learnt from Ashish Chanchlani's evolution as a personal brand. A few of them are given here.

CREATE YOUR OWN IDENTITY

For many people, their identity is defined by community, location, family or job. But a few create such strong self-identities that the community, family and company take pride in them. Ashish is one such person. During the terrible partition of India in 1947, many from the Sindhi community migrated to Ulhasnagar, Mumbai. They came as penniless refugees, having lost everything. One of them was Ashish's grandfather, Assandas Chanchlani.

Interested in movies, Ashish's grandfather began his career as a manager at a cinema hall owned by a Parsi gentleman. His employer was greatly impressed by Assandas' determination and loyaty. When he moved to the US to live with his daughter, he handed over the theatre to Assandas. Sindhis are known for their business sense. With hard work, Assandas turned one theatre into two. The business flourished, and the Chanchlani family saw their fortunes grow.

Often, children born into a wealthy family are ill-prepared to manage money. This results in bad decision-making and puts the family wealth at risk. To nurture a sense of responsibility in his children, Assandas pulled his sons Anil and Ashok into the business at an early age. Ashish's father, Anil, was a talented artist and wanted to become a painter. However, in order to focus on the family business, he sacrificed his dream. An introverted child, Anil was bullied as a boy. Ultimately, he learnt to fight back and stand up for himself. Ashish says, 'My father has a very strong personality. Whosoever bullied him actually prepared him for bigger things in life.' In time, Anil Chanchlani developed a larger vision for the family business and expanded it to a chain of theatres. Today, he owns the famous Miraj Ashok Anil Multiplex in Ulhasnagar.

It is common in affluent families to be overprotective of their children. This was the case with Ashish as well. His family treated him with excessive care and indulgence. Bullies typically target children who are defenseless and vulnerable. Considering Ashish to be something of a baby, some of the children in school began to bully him.

He faced other challenges as well. Because of his family's social status, there were many judgments made about him by those around him. Some of his realtives commented on how he ate, spoke and dressed. A few even considered him incapable of charting his own course in life.

Ashish became increasingly frustrated with his situation. He respected his father for having created his own identity beyond the influence of his grandfather. Anil Chanchlani would often tell his son, '*Apne kaam se aapko jo izzat milti hain, woh apne father ke naam se nahi milti.*' ('The dignity and prestige you will get from your own work, you cannot get from your father's name.') Like his father, Ashish too, wanted to be known by his work and not by the family tag. He continues to believe that if children of affluent families are dependent on the family name and influence, they may open one or two doors, but their individual personality will lose its worth. If left alone without the family buttress, they will find themselves helpless. On the other hand, if a person prepares themselves to survive and thrive based on their self-identity, many doors will open even without family influence. Ashish says, 'Neither did I want to use my father's name, nor his money. I wanted to stand on my own feet.'

By Class IX, Ashish had decided to take control of the situation. He began taking on the bullies. Without the knowledge of his parents, he also learnt to ride the cycle at his maternal grandmother's home. He fell many times, but hid his bruises. In time, his parents realised that a life of privilege would not quench their son's fire to achieve something independently. Today, Ashish says, 'My father has played a big role in what I am today. He appreciated my thoughts and gave me a lot of moral support when I was trying to discover myself.'

Today, Ashish is one of the most powerful content creators in the digital world. Many youngsters consider him a role model. Top-notch brands approach him to endorse their products. Bollywood stars collaborate with him for their film promotions. Like Sanjeev Bikhchandani, Rajkumar Hirani, Ashish Hemrajani, and others, Ashish Chanchlani has become a famous face of the new-age Sindhi community. 'I am grateful to my followers, who loved my work and helped me build my identity,' Ashish says.

DESIGN YOUR PATH WITH YOUR DEDICATION

James Clear, author of the book *Atomic Habits*, said, 'Rome wasn't built in a day, but they were laying bricks every hour. You don't have to do it all today. Just lay a brick. That's how you build an empire.' In the same way, Ashish built his digital content empire by working on small content ideas every day.

While in engineering college, Ashish failed one of the subjects in his first year. His dream of becoming an actor was not going anywhere and his academic downfall caused him great disappointment. He told his father, 'I don't want to do engineering. Maybe I made a wrong choice. Acting is my passion, and I should have tried to become an actor, not an engineer.' His father listened to him patiently, then said, 'I know you are frustrated. If you want to become an actor, go ahead, I will not stop you. However, you are a fighter. You don't leave things incomplete. So, finish your engineering. Life will find a way for you.' Ashish felt motivated by his father's words and decided to pursue both his dream and his studies.

A month later, Ashish was scrolling through his Facebook feed and saw a short 6.5-second video of a man called David Lopez. It was a very funny Vine video. Ashish searched for Vine and found that it was a social media app where people could post 6.5-second videos. Immediately, he thought of creating his own Vine videos. Ashish copied his first three Vine video ideas from international Viners. Sadly, all of them got tons of negative comments. This brutal experience taught Ashish that he had to stop copying Western ideas and make something Indian. He made his first original Vine video on how girls love Maggi noodles. It was a success. From then on, he made other Vines with desi flavours. Simultaneously, he joined the college event committee and hosted many events, which helped improve his speaking and acting skills.

While in college, Ashish started his YouTube channel Ashish Chanchlani Vines, using 'Vines' in tribute to the social media app Vine on which he had begun his journey. After finishing his engineering course, Ashish told his father that he wished to join a professional course to improve his acting skills. While researching acting schools, Ashish found that famous actors like Manoj Bajpayee, Shah Rukh Khan and Varun Dhawan were all alumni of Barry John Acting Studio, so he decided to go there. However, commuting from Ulhasnagar to the acting school in Andheri was painful. Ashish's day would begin at 5 a.m. to catch the train at 6 a.m. By the time he got home again, it was close to midnight.

Though Ashish enjoyed the acting classes, his personal life and health were being adversely affected by the 5–6-hour daily commute. Exhausted, it was difficult to give his 100 per cent at the acting classes. He decided to leave the course within a month. Filled with guilt at having wasted his father's money and not completing a course he had insisted on doing, he promised himself that one day he would return the fee money to his father. But in that one month of training, Ashish realised that he could improve his acting skills by practising. So he decided to watch acts of his favourite stars and practise on his own.

From his childhood, Akshay Kumar has been a role model for Ashish. 'His transition from action to comedy was amazing. His comic timing is brilliant. I love his persona and admire his journey,' he says. Ashish also learnt comedy skills by watching Bollywood stars like Govinda and Arshad Warsi. He repeatedly watched Amitabh Bachchan's films to understand his dialogue delivery. He also watched numerous English movies and is a great admirer of South Indian cinema, watching the films in their original languages. Ashish says, 'Bollywood does make great films. However, many of the films made in southern languages such as Tamil, Telugu, Kannada and Malayalam are brilliant. They respect cinema, and they don't take their audience for granted. I love them for daring to make different movies, their immense talent pool, the dialogues and the presentation.'

Taking inspiration from various stars, Ashish continued to practise and make his YouTube videos. Although he was not making any money, he was happy that thousands of people were watching his videos and giving him feedback. Every day, Ashish worked 14–18 hours on acting and planning his videos and polishing his acting skills. He also took interaction with his audience very seriously.

In 2018, Ashish collaborated with Akshay Kumar for the promotion of the film *Gold*. He says, 'It was a dream-come-true opportunity for me. I was happy to know that his son watches my videos.' Ashish also got very emotional when Rajkummar Rao appreciated his work. There was a time when Ashish had been just another guy from Ulhasnagar. Today, Bollywood stars follow him on social media and like his videos. Undoubtedly, Ashish has come a long way from being bullied in the school playground.

TREAT OTHERS WITH RESPECT AND AFFECTION

When you treat others with respect and affection, appreciate and value their work, you build strong relationships and get the best out of them. Since childhood, Ashish's mother, Deepa Chanchlani, had taught him the value of respecting and appreciating others. Now, even when Ashish collects a courier at home, he appreciates the courier delivery person's work, and thanks him without fail. 'It doesn't matter whether I am a celebrity or the other person is a common man, I have been taught to respect everyone. However, if the other person is rude, I can't be good with that person, even if they are the biggest celebrity on the planet.'

Just as his family upbringing taught Ashish that people feel good when they are respected, his own rejections taught him that people feel bad when they are humiliated. 'During the early days of my career, I appeared for ten auditions and was rejected in all of them. In nine of the auditions, I was treated like a human being, and was politely told they were looking for someone thinner and more confident. I was overweight and underconfident. So I was fine with those genuine rejections. However, in the tenth rejection, I was treated really harshly,' Ashish recalls.

The tenth audition was taken by Siddhant Chaturvedi, who played the character of MC Sher in *Gully Boy*. While Siddhant himself was nice to those auditioning, the girl with him was rude. Ashish says, 'I don't like people who consider themselves classy and others worthless.' He was not then in a position to say anything to the girl, so he silently digested the insult. But he made up his mind that he would become so skilled in his craft that the casting director of the film would himself offer him a role one day. Then he would tell him that this girl on his team should have treated strugglers as humans. From then on, Ashish stopped going for auditions.

Because of his friendly nature, Ashish was able to attract people to support his journey. His cousins Jashan Sirwani and Tanish Sirwani were his initial supporters. Ashish says, 'My brothers believed in my vision and stood with me when everyone doubted me.' Then, Ashish's childhood friend Akash Dodeja (popularly known as Jadoo), joined him in the journey. Ashish's college friend Naveen Dudani had always believed in Ashish's talent. He introduced Ashish to many people, including Kunal Chhabhria, who did auditions for TV serials and possessed deep knowledge of video creation. He taught Ashish how to execute interesting ideas and helped to improve the quality of his videos. In 2017, Kunal joined Ashish's team.

That same year, Ashish met Simran through a fan. Since then, she has been an important character in Ashish's videos. As none of his team members were trained actors, Ashish guided them in areas like oration, articulation, presentation, etc. Ashish says, 'My team has given me many interesting ideas, which took my content to another level. I am happy that through our videos, they have also become popular, and many opportunities have opened up for them.'

Ashish started his YouTube journey in late 2014 and earned nothing for two years. He says, 'It was a quite frustrating period for me. I didn't want to take money from my father. So I kept my bigger ideas on hold and created simple videos using my mobile phone.' In the third year, a few thousand rupees started coming in every month from YouTube. 'This amount was minuscule but helped me in experimenting with some ideas,' he explains.

In 2017, Ashish got his first brand deal. Someone from Star Sports called him to ask whether he would like to create an Instagram video for an India versus Pakistan match. Ashish asked what he would get in return. He was offered ₹70,000. In 2016, Ashish had not made that much in the whole year, and now he was earning ₹70,000 for just one video? Deliriously happy, he began to dance in his room. When the money came, he said to his mother, '*Mummy, finally meri mehnat ke paise aa gaye.*' (Mummy, finally I have received the reward of my hard work.) As a gesture of respect, he gave her the money.

Since then, Ashish has received numerous high-value opportunities. Funnily enough, his fanboy moment came when he got the opportunity to collaborate with Marvel Studios. Since childhood, Ashish has been a die-hard fan of Marvel movies. Learning of his love for Marvel movies through his Instagram videos, the Marvel India team contacted him to interview the *Avengers: Infinity War* director and cast in Singapore. Ashish was so excited he could not sleep for the next two days. Being both an influencer and a Marvel fan, Ashish's interaction with the

Marvel team was one of love and respect. Perhaps the Marvel team was happy with Ashish too, for the next year, he was invited to the red carpet premiere of *Avengers: Endgame* in Los Angeles. Ashish says, 'At the Los Angeles event, I was more confident than at the Singapore event, and my ability to interact with these stars was much improved. I will always remain thankful to Marvel for giving me these precious opportunities.'

In this journey to stardom, one thing has remained constant in Ashish—his humility and down-to-earth attitude. He believes that fame is temporary and ego destroys relationships. For him, the most important thing is the love people give him.

THINK FROM YOUR AUDIENCE'S PERSPECTIVE

The most important asset in an influencer's journey is the audience. If the audience stops following an influencer, they are quickly back to ground zero. In order to create a strong bond with their audience, an influencer must be truthful with them.

To be honest with the audience, first and foremost an influencer must genuinely like his field. As Ashish says, 'I have loved comedy since childhood. Whenever I opened my mouth, people enjoyed my content, voice and accent. So I felt my strength lay in making others laugh. Another reason I love comedy is because it is like chocolate. From cake to shake, you can have anything with chocolate. Similarly, if you give any message with comedy, people lap it up.' But even within comedy, there are various styles. Ashish understands that his strength lies in skit-based comedy, where he can showcase his acting skills. So he has focused on skits rather than stand-up comedy or the like.

YouTube is filled with numerous comedy videos. In such a crowded space, standing out and making a name for yourself is not easy. Ashish says, 'I never thought of standing out; I just thought of giving my 100 per cent. I put my heart into every video I create.' Every YouTuber has a different style of creating content, based on their background. Having been born and brought up in Ulhasnagar, Ashish's accent and intonation have a touch of the Sindhi language, which adds an attractive element to his performances.

The most difficult part about being a comedian is the fact that one has to deliver fresh content all the time. Ashish says, 'I look at topics from a fresh perspective. So, even if a topic or scenario is common, we try to differentiate our script through our fresh perspective, dialogues and execution.'

Over time, audience tastes change, sometimes quite dramatically, so content creators have to keep themselves updated. Working in Ashish's favour is that he understands millennials well and makes relatable content. He believes in learning what is happening around him and staying connected with his audience. He regularly posts stories on Instagram and honestly tells his audience what he is going through and what he cannot understand. 'My audience is my family. They are the ones who constantly support me through their messages and advice.'

It is really important for a content creator to let the audience know that he is listening to them. As Ashish says, 'There are so many instances where I have made videos because my audience suggested something to me.' He observes everything around him and then delivers his observations with a funny twist.

Because Ashish has millions of followers, many brands reach out to him for collaboration. Before accepting any collaboration opportunity, Ashish and his team undertake extensive research on the brand. They try to understand how many people are using the brand already. From existing customers, they try to understand the advantages and disadvantages of the brand's product. Sometimes, Ashish and his team even use the product. Having satisfied themselves, they check whether the brand will accept the team's content idea. If everything aligns, only then does Ashish move ahead. As a personal policy, he never pushes his audience towards addictions, so he never collaborates with liquor, tobacco or gambling-related brands, even when the offers are lucrative.

Interestingly, Ashish's ability to break the fourth wall makes his brand collaborations appealing. The fourth wall refers to the boundary between stage and audience, a gap between fiction and reality. Applying this technique in his videos, Ashish acknowledges that he is talking about a particular brand because it is a paid engagement. 'Breaking the fourth wall makes the audience more interested. Simultaneously, they consider you genuine,' Ashish says.

On one occasion, Vivo engaged a couple of influencers for YouTube live sessions. In one of the sessions, the audience felt like they were watching an advertisement, and that video got many dislikes. On the other hand, Ashish broke the fourth wall and told his audience upfront that this brand has supported him, and he wanted their support. He asked them to write comments like, *Wah kya influencer hain*! (Wow! What an influencer he is!) whenever they liked something. People appreciated his genuineness and he got many comments. The engagement was fruitful for the brand. Ashish says, 'Don't hide. Be honest with your audience. People appreciate transparency and authenticity.'

BUILD AND REBUILD YOUR CONFIDENCE

Creative people are adventurous and exploratory. They see things that others usually do not. To turn their imagination into reality, creative people have to show a lot of confidence. Ashish learnt early in life that if he wanted to move ahead in his field, his most important asset would be confidence. As creative people try new things, they have to confront both doubt and rejection. In the face of these, it is easy to lose one's self-confidence. It happened to Ashish quite a few times and he had to rebuild his confidence over and over again.

After dropping out of the course at the Barry John Acting Studio, Ashish joined his family business. He became a victim to a boring routine that made his life mechanical. He was not able to give 100 per cent to his passion, acting, and thus faced great frustration. In 2015, Ashish happened to watch the film *Tamasha*, starring Ranbir Kapoor. It was about pursuing what you love against the tide of an ordinary life. He cried after watching the film. It inspired him to follow his heart. At the time, he had 2,000 followers. He felt that if so many people were watching his content, he must be doing something interesting, and the craft should be taken to the next level. He decided to give 100 per cent to his passion.

Whether we like it or not, the sad reality of this world is that money is required for relevance. So, though video creation was mentally satisfying, Ashish was not making any money. In 2016, he felt that beyond achieving a certain popularity, nothing was happening on YouTube. He told his father that he wanted to try in Bollywood. Even a small role would help him earn. His father replied, 'People are appreciating your work on YouTube. You have an opportunity to become a king in your field. Then why do you want to stand in queues for auditions in Bollywood? The world is changing. Soon, everyone will come towards digital.' Ashish remembers, 'After a few years I felt that Goddess Saraswati had been sitting on my father's tongue then. Today, I can see the world is moving towards digital. Web series, Bollywood, audiences; everything seems to be gravitating towards digital.'

Bolstering his confidence, Ashish kept on creating his videos. In 2017, some brand deals happened, and money started coming in. By 2018, Ashish had become one of India's topmost content creators and was in the news for his rise. He was happy to see people had started liking his work.

However, destiny wanted him to learn some new lessons about life. In 2019, Ashish uploaded the video 'Cricket Gully Gully Ki' ('cricket in every alley'). Within 6 hours, it had received 50,000 dislikes. Ashish was bewildered and could not understand why people disliked it. His heart was broken. For almost a month, he remained deeply frustrated. To pull himself out of self-doubt, he reviewed his previous work and the journey. He felt that if he had been able to get this far, he has something in him that his audience liked. To make a comeback, he got back to work, determined to give his 1,000 per cent.

His next video, 'Student Life: Bollywood VS Reality', performed beyond Ashish's expectations and broke records. By now, the previous video that had got numerous dislikes was getting thousands of likes! Ashish was surprised by this changing wave. While introspecting, he found that before the 'Cricket Gully Gully Ki' video, Ashish had announced that he was coming up with an interesting video on cricket. Prior to this, he had never made such announcements. Perhaps the announcement had raised certain expectations for the audience, which were not met. Later, when people watched the same video, without expectations, their reaction was different. Interestingly, in the next two years, this video received around 45 million views and close to 2 million likes. The number of initial dislikes suddenly looked minuscule.

When you become an influencer, along with your work, you are required to also manage any controversies created around you. Back in 2013, annoyed that his favourite IPL team was losing to MS Dhoni's side, Ashish tweeted to a friend that MS Dhoni was the most overrated player. At the time, Ashish was a college student, and this a casual conversation on social media. In 2020, someone re-tweeted Ashish's 2013 tweet about MS Dhoni. It went viral and did not go down well with MS Dhoni fans. They began trolling Ashish mercilessly. Ashish deleted his 2013 tweet, but then someone started circulating a screenshot of it. Ashish tried to clarify by giving examples of his many other tweets written about MS Dhoni. But the hateful messages kept on coming. This incident created a lot of stress for Ashish. Later, his fans defended him. Around the same time, other random controversies started appearing around Ashish. He did not know who was behind all this negativity.

Then COVID-19 hit the world. An unprecedented lockdown followed in India. Then came the death of Sushant Singh Rajput, the young film star. The combined effect of all these events increased Ashish's feelings of stress. He lost interest in doing things, giving in to hopelessness and fear. For almost a month, he would cry for hours. He felt that his career was finished. He spiralled into depression. His family and friends tried to motivate him, with little success. Unsure of his comeback, Ashish thought to inform his fans through a YouTube Live session about his depression and taking a break.

Sometimes, when you are in trouble, God speaks to you through signs. Something similar happened with Ashish. Gaur Gopal Das, an Indian spiritual leader, watched Ashish's live video and called him that night. He told Ashish he had watched the video by chance and felt that Ashish was in some deep trouble. Ashish began to cry on the phone, expressing his fears. For the next three days, Gaur Gopal Das counselled Ashish and helped him regain his equilibrium. Ashish says today, 'I had met Gaur Gopal Dasji at my TEDx talk in 2016. I had taken his blessings at the event. It was very kind of him to remember and call me when I was going through a tough phase.' After talking to Gaur Gopal Das, Ashish felt like God was standing with him, and he was ready to confront any challenge.

After a three-month break, Ashish returned with a new video, 'Raksha Bandhan'. It crossed millions of views within a few hours and became the #1 trending video on YouTube. Since then, Ashish has created many viral videos and acquired millions of new subscribers. In 2021, Ashish's video 'Sasta Biig Bosss | Parody' and 'Office Exam Aur Vaccine', broke all the viewership records. In 2022, he created a spoof of Shark Tank India called 'Sasta Shark Tank'. By April 2024, the video had received more than 77 million views.

Ashish says, 'Gaur Gopal Dasji called me when I was not doing well. Now, when I am doing well, I keep sending him thank you messages.'

IN CONCLUSION

Within a short period, Ashish has covered a phenomenal journey. He says, 'This journey wouldn't have been possible without YouTube. It gave me a chance to showcase my talent to millions of people.' He adds, '*Is journey main, maine bahut kuch seekha hai. Main ek bachche se aadmi bana hu* (On this journey, I have learnt a lot. From a boy, I have become a man). Thanks to YouTube!'

Instead of resting on his laurels, Ashish is restless to create better content for his audience. He says, 'I want to make content that places India with the world's best.' Besides acting, Ashish is also polishing his directorial skills. 'I want to direct and bring out some ground-breaking movies,' he says.

The most inspiring part of Ashish's journey is that he has not only created his own identity, but that he has inspired many others to do so. Taking inspiration and guidance from him, many youngsters have started their YouTube channels, Instagram pages and content agencies, and some of them, including his sister Muskan Chanchlani, have become quite popular. Ashish says, 'I feel very happy when I see these youngsters doing so well. I might have played some small role initially, but it is their hard work that has made them what they are today. I am very proud of them.'

Nothing in this world remains static, and it will be interesting to see how brand Ashish Chanchlani evolves with time, assuming ever-new dimensions.

Perspectives from Ashish Chanchlani

- The risk and tension of entrepreneurship is often double that of a regular job. But the fun is also four times as much. It gives you a chance to discover yourself and become a leader.
- Never doubt yourself. Be 100 per cent loyal to yourself. Stop making excuses and blaming others for your failures. Own up to your mistakes.
- Avoid having a God complex. You cannot always be right. Listen to others. You never know. They might have a better and more intelligent perspective than you.
- Be flexible. Accept that the world is changing, and you have to change accordingly.
- Sometimes, life brings a dark phase. Don't lose hope. Do not let temporary emotions direct permanent decisions. Even if your life seems dark now, it will not be so forever. Don't take any hard, stupid or dark decisions due to short-term pain.
- In challenging situations, don't sympathise with yourself. Be strong and fight the situation. Struggle creates a better version of you.
- Treat your followers as people, not numbers. People's emotions and love take you ahead in life. Respect them.
- There will always be people who love you and those who hate you. Focus on those who love you and give you constructive feedback. You can't do much about people who hate you.

KABITA SINGH

KABITA SINGH

From Unknown Homemaker to Acclaimed Chef

I would like to be remembered as someone who did the best she could with the talent she had.

—J.K. Rowling

The 2007 animated film *Ratatouille* is considered a masterpiece. The film won the Academy Award for Best Animated Feature. It was later voted one of the hundred greatest motion pictures of the twenty-first century by a poll of international critics, conducted by the BBC. The film's protagonist is Remy, a young rat with a deep passion for cooking, who dreams of emulating France's most popular chef, Auguste Gusteau, whose famous saying is: *Anyone can cook*. But Remy is unable to fulfil his ambitions because he is a rat. Still determined, Remy finds his way into Gusteau's restaurant by concealing himself inside the hat of a garbage boy, Alfredo Linguini. Thus hidden, Remy helps Linguini cook amazing meals, which prove enormously successful.

You are probably wondering what all this has to do with our story? Stay with us... the story is just beginning.

When Kabita Singh, a mother of two, had watched *Ratatouille* as a children's film, she was unaware that this film would give her a purpose in life. In 2014, Kabita's son had just started preschool and she wanted to utilise her time productively. Taking up a job was not a viable option as Kabita did not wish to compromise on her household responsibilities. Therefore, she decided to start a YouTube channel of food recipes that would be so simple that 'anyone could cook'. Today, her channel Kabita's Kitchen, has become one of the most popular digital properties in India. At the 2024 National Creators Award, Kabita received the Best Creator in the Food Category honour from the Prime Minister of India, Narendra Modi. As of April 2024, more than 18 million people follow Kabita on various social media platforms such as YouTube, Facebook and Instagram. She has also launched a range of spices under the brand 'Kabita's Kitchen Masala Mix'.

But it was not as if Kabita made it big overnight. She had her quota of painful days and sleepless nights. This is then the story of Kabita, an unknown homemaker, who has become one of the most prominent digital chefs in India.

THE BEGINNING

Born into a Kolkata-based middle-class business family, Kabita grew up in a family of seven, including her four siblings. The home had just one room, attached to a kitchen. So Kabita got exposed to cooking at a very early age. While carefully observing her mother cook, Kabita would ask questions about the spices, ingredients and recipes. When she was in Class VII, her mother divided the housework among the children. Kabita had the responsibility of assisting her mother in cooking the family meals. By the time Kabita was in Class XI, she had assumed full responsibility of the kitchen.

While studying for her B. Com degree, Kabita would also manage responsibilities at home and tutor children in the locality. Post graduation, she got a job as a sales executive at ICICI Bank at a monthly salary of ₹3,500. Later, she joined IL&FS Group, and her salary went up to ₹17,000. As a middle-class girl, she was thought to be doing well in her career, and marriage proposals began coming in. However, prospective grooms inevitably asked for large dowries, so the matter never moved forward.

In 2008, Kabita's family friend, Binod Singh, suggested she meet his brother-in-law, Manish. At the time, Manish worked as a software engineer in the UK. He had come to India for work. He told Binod he really was not interested in getting married just then. Nevertheless, he travelled to Kolkata due to family pressure. When the two met, Kabita told him she preferred to live in Kolkata, and turned down the proposal. Manish did not care for her sense of humour, so he too, said no. Impasse. But, as they say, marriages are made in heaven. To everyone's surprise, six months later, they both agreed to the marriage.

On 4 March 2009, married to Manish, Kabita moved to the UK. There, she was disappointed with the Indian food available and began watching Indian recipes on YouTube. While watching the videos of others, she began to dream of starting her own channel someday.

By April 2014, Kabita and Manish had returned to India and were living in Pune. Kabita had given up her career to focus on their son. When he started preschool, she suddenly had time on her hands. She shared her desire to work with Manish, who advised, 'Don't work for money. Rather, do something that will make you feel happy and satisfied.'

Kabita's neighbour and friend from her UK days, Shilpa Ruchandani, used to run a YouTube channel on painting and drawing. She was looking to hire someone for video editing work. Kabita felt the job of a video editor would prepare her to start her own YouTube channel in the future. Knowing Kabita's aspirations, Shilpa suggested she start the channel right away and learn the skills on the go.

Kabita borrowed a tripod from Shilpa and shot a video of bhindi fry, a dish she was cooking for lunch. That evening, when Manish came back from the office, he appreciated Kabita's effort. Over the next four days, Kabita learnt video editing on YouTube. Then it took her another ten days to edit her first video. Wherever she felt stuck, Manish helped her with his technical competencies. On 2 November 2014, she uploaded her first video on the channel, Kabita's Kitchen.

There are many valuable lessons to be learned from the evolution of Kabita Singh as a personal brand. A few of them are shared here.

HAVE PATIENCE, THE BREAKOUT MOMENT WILL COME

Many of you will have heard the story of the stonecutter who wanted to split a big rock. He took his hammer and started to hit it. He did not make even a scratch. He hit the rock again and again. Not even a crack appeared. But he continued hammering. People saw him get no results and laughed at him. But the stonecutter kept hammering. He knew that though he could not see any immediate effects of his actions, he was making progress. He continued his hammering. After more than 700 strikes, the rock split in half. The moral of the story is that constant pressure applied to the rock finally broke it.

Like the stonecutter, Kabita remained patient. Starting with her first video, she uploaded one recipe every day. But she hardly got any traction. Only a few views came from her friends and family members. After two months, someone commented on one of her videos and asked her to share the recipe for chicken kathi roll. Kabita learnt the recipe, simplified it and prepared the dish for the first time in her life. She asked Manish to try it. He loved the taste. Happily, Kabita uploaded the video and messaged the person who had asked for the recipe. She received no response.

She kept posting her recipe videos, and six months later, she received $1 in her account. She discovered that Google Adsense pays YouTubers once they achieve a certain threshold in terms of videos and views. To celebrate her first earning from her passion, she organised a pizza party at home. Kabita remembers, 'This was my first earning from YouTube, so the feeling was very different. For an income of $1, I spent ₹2,200 on a pizza party.'

But the journey was not easy. Kabita's initial eighty-nine videos did not get much of a response. But the break-out moment had arrived. The next day was to be the beginning of her turnaround.

Traditionally, gulab jamun is made using khoya, a milk extract used to make sweets. However, instead of khoya, Kabita used bread. On 3 December 2016, she uploaded her ninetieth video, the recipe for bread gulab jamun. The video went viral. Within a month, it was receiving nearly 100,000 views daily. Due to the popularity of this video, other videos on the channel also started gaining traction. On 19 February 2017, Kabita's Kitchen crossed the 1-million-subscriber mark. In the next eight months, the channel crossed 2 million subscribers. Kabita was delighted to see the affection and responses she was getting from her audience.

Until then, Kabita had posted videos as and when she had the time. But she soon realised she would have to create a timetable so that viewers knew when to expect her videos. This would increase audience interaction. For the next three years, Kabita posted a video every Tuesday, Thursday and Saturday. Interestingly, the videos posted according to the timetable got higher views than those posted randomly. By January 2020, Kabita's Kitchen had around 6 million subscribers.

Then, in March 2020, the national COVID-19 lockdown started. As many bachelors and working women were at home, Kabita started getting many requests for beginner-level recipes. She posted recipes showing how to cook roti, sabzi, dal, rice, chole chawal, etc. Along with these recipes, she also posted more accessible versions of snacks and sweets. By October 2020, the channel had crossed the milestone of 9 million subscribers.

Kabita says, 'Many people start YouTube channels, but they stop posting videos if they don't get the expected response in the initial fifteen to twenty videos. The breakout moment takes some time to come, but it definitely comes if one is patient and consistent.'

THE CONTENT WAS, IS, AND WILL ALWAYS BE KING

In January 1996, Bill Gates wrote an essay titled 'Content is King', published on the Microsoft website. In this essay, he said that one of the exciting things about the Internet is that anyone with a PC and a modem can publish whatever content they create. He also mentioned that the internet allows information to be distributed worldwide at basically zero marginal cost to the publisher. But he also expected to see intense competition and failure, as well as success, in all categories of popular content.

Food content is undoubtedly a highly competitive category. Everyone has an opinion on food! Tarla Dalal was once the only Indian celebrity in the world of cooking. She wrote over a hundred cookbooks. Suddenly, many other cookbook writers began to emerge. Then came Sanjeev Kapoor, who transformed the profession of chef into something respectable and even glamorous. Suddenly, many TV channels started creating cookery shows of their own. Then came the YouTube era, and many chefs tried creating food channels, but few achieved substantial user growth and engagement.

You must be thinking, so how did Kabita become a household name?

Kabita says, 'When people think of starting a YouTube channel, they think about a fancy camera, lighting, an interesting set-up, video promotion and other packaging factors. These things are important, but the most important thing is the content. Users watch your video because of the content, and it has to be relevant and different. If you are confident about your content, everything else will fall into place. If your content is well-received and appreciated, then the ride will be smooth.'

To make her content relevant and different from others, Kabita focussed on a classic branding strategy—identify a niche and become an expert in it. Kabita had seen thousands of food videos and found that although they were well-packaged, attention to detail was missing. In most of the dishes, the chefs use a lot of ingredients. Also, cooking timing and temperatures varied for different dishes. If not adequately cooked, food can taste awful. In TV and digital shows, chefs usually said, 'Heat the food for some time', or 'use a pinch of spice', or 'use 1/2 a cup of oil and 3/4 cup of yogurt', and so on. Many viewers do not understand what 'some time' or 'a pinch' means, or which cup size is relevant to the context. If they add extra spices or cook for a shorter time, or use the wrong spoon or cup to measure, the taste will not be as expected.

Kabita decided to differentiate her content by covering even the most minor details of cooking. She positioned Kabita's Kitchen as a channel for beginners and bachelors. She decided to feature easy, instant recipes that 'anyone can cook', with ingredients readily available at home or at a nearby grocery store. While preparing the recipes, she noted every detail from utensils required to ingredients, quantities, methodology and even the intensity of the flame. She referred to these notes while preparing her video and doing the voice-over.

While attention to detail is good, it can also make videos boring. Kabita likes the speaking style of Chef Sanjeev Kapoor and Chef Harpal Singh Sokhi. Following them and utilising her past teaching experience, Kabita has developed her own explanation style in Hindi, as her audience can relate to it easily. Also, she keeps the cooking set-up homely and straightforward so people find it relatable. The relatability of the environment adds to the comfort level of her viewers. Because of the simplicity of her content, Kabita has received many exciting comments from her audience, such as, 'You made a girl who could not make tea into someone looked up to in the family circle for good food.'

NEVER SHY AWAY FROM HARD WORK

Struggle sets the stage for success. People know Kabita as an influencer with millions of followers. But to achieve this milestone, she has had to put in a great deal of effort. When she began her journey, she knew how to cook, but she didn't know anything about video creation. Through YouTube, she has learnt to work on camera, handle lighting, edit her videos and do colour correction. As she was not trained to do this professionally, the initial months were tough. She had limited time to capture the cooking process, and many times, the process was not satisfactory and needed to be repeated, resulting in a lot of wastage. It took a lot of time.

YouTubers have to consistently upload videos. If they fail to do so, their relevance drops quickly, overrun by the fierce competition. To enhance audience delight, Kabita has to come up with new recipes continuously. She reads every comment from her audience to understand what they want. Every week, she checks Google Trends to understand what recipes people are looking for. She also watches videos of other cooking channels to get a sense of what dishes people have enjoyed and appreciated. Kabita observes, 'If someone has already cooked a dish, cooking it the same way does not help. So I think how a particular dish can be created differently.'

Kabita researches the origins of various dishes on Wikipedia and Google. She studies how a dish can be prepared in an authentic way, in restaurant style or effortlessly. Some dishes have expensive ingredients, so she looks for cheaper alternatives that are easily available in the market. Sometimes, she even brings in a dish from a restaurant and analyses its ingredients and taste experience. Every dish research process takes two or three days. After this, if Kabita does not like a dish, she restarts the recipe research process with another dish.

Kabita has a nine-year-old son and a three-year-old-daughter and manages the house. Juggling her multiple responsibilities is often very challenging. As a mother, she feels that she should give all her time to her kids, and as a chef, she feels she must prepare something new for her audience every few days. To achieve a work–life balance, she has made changes to her daily schedule. For example, she works when her son is at school or when both her kids are asleep. Another challenge is that the apartment gets a lot of street noise during the day, hence doing voice-overs is impossible in the daytime. Nor can she record and work in a professional studio as that would compromise the quality time she spends with the family. As a workaround, she works on her voice-over late at night, usually between 11.30 p.m. and 2 a.m. If the family plans to go on holiday, Kabita puts in double shifts to create extra videos in the week before the vacation.

Kabita does not have many friends, and because of her busy schedule, she is unable to participate in social gatherings or outings like other homemakers. It is not an easy road to travel. She says, 'Life is all about choices. If you have chosen an unconventional path, you should not compare yourself with people on a conventional path.' She is passionate about cooking and enjoys her work, so she is able to make time for the essential things in her life.

PROTECT THE TRUST YOU HAVE EARNED

Influencers have vast subscriber bases, massive visibility and an appeal that cuts across different types of audiences. Hence they are attractive to advertisers, who approach them with partnership deals. Every business needs to be profitable, and the same is true of YouTube channels. But there is a catch here. Audiences follow influencers because of the trust factor. If influencers succumb too deeply to the lure of brand deals, they can damage their relationship with the audience. Kabita has been very selective about her brand associations. She says, 'For any influencer, reputation is the most powerful asset. Years are spent building a name and reputation. One should only associate with brands one has used or believes in.'

As soon as Kabita touched a subscriber base of 100,000, brands began approaching her. She discussed it with her husband, Manish, and they decided not to take any brand deals until the subscriber base reached 2 million. Kabita says, 'I started this channel with a purpose, to help my audience with food recipes. If I overthink brand associations, I will get diverted from my purpose.' To ensure that Kabita gives 100 per cent to her creativity and doesn't get distracted by commerce with brands, Manish manages Kabita's brand endorsements and finances. He says, 'When someone is small, the powerful party dominates the discussion. If we had started taking advertising opportunities with a small subscriber base, brands would have dominated our content. Also, if someone starts endorsements early, the audience might not take them seriously.' To have an equal say in the creative process, Manish and Kabita preferred to wait.

Kabita integrated the first brand in her video after reaching a subscriber base of 3 million. Since then, she has worked with many renowned brands, including Nestlé, Dabur, Britannia, Marico, Complan and others. She believes that any brand integration involves not only the two contracting parties, the brand and the creator, but also the audience as a third party. Endorsements help the audience in making choices. So, it is essential that all three parties benefit. As a principle, Kabita never creates a video for a brand. She makes a video for her audience. If she finds that a brand can be integrated into the video authentically, then she does so. Else, she politely declines the opportunity. For instance, when Kabita was offered a lucrative deal for a full-brand video, at three times her usual fee, Manish turned it down.

He says, 'We also prefer to work with brands who treat creators as partners and give them the freedom to strategise the concept.' For instance, some time back, HealthifyMe, a digital health and wellness platform, partnered with Kabita to develop healthy recipes. The objective of the brand was to get some visibility and achieve at least 100 app downloads. Manish explains that just one video doesn't make an impact. Rather a campaign with several videos helps to establish a connection. He suggested to the brand that they do a 360-degree campaign rather than just one video and also associate the campaign with New Year resolutions, rather than the original campaign timeline of November to January. The outcome was fantastic. Kabita's video achieved over 10 million views, and the brand over 5,000 app downloads. Also, Kabita got visibility for her recipes on the HealthifyMe platform.

Kabita says, 'Fans follow creators because of the trust factor. Before saying yes to any brand association, I try the product, and only if I am satisfied and think it will be useful for my audience do I say yes.' Apart from the type of integration and kind of brand, Kabita is cautious about the frequency of brand-related videos. Though she receives many association-related inquiries, she does only 25 per cent of videos with brand integration in any month. The rest, 75 per cent of the videos have no brand integration.

HAVE SOMEONE TO ENCOURAGE YOU

George Burton Adams once said, 'There is no such thing as a "self-made" person. We are made up of thousands of others. Everyone who has ever done a kind deed for us, or spoken one word of encouragement to us, has entered into the make-up of our character and of our thoughts, as well as our success.' To the external world, Kabita is a very popular personal brand, but behind the scenes, a few people have inspired and supported her through the ups and downs of her journey.

Kabita's mother has been her first teacher and a source of inspiration for her. Kabita's mother loves to experiment with food. Whenever Kabita calls her, she tells Kabita about her cooking experiments and innovations with dishes. 'My mother's passion for cooking, even in old age, energises me to keep delighting my audience with new recipes,' Kabita says with a smile.

Another person who has played a crucial role in Kabita's journey is her husband, Manish, who hails from a farming family. In his childhood, he was a talented cricketer and wanted to build a career in the game. However, the family's constrained finances did not permit him to pursue this dream. He decided to focus on academics and get a good job that would support his family. At the age of eighteen, Manish's elder brother joined the army, allowing Manish to focus on his studies. In due course, he earned a bachelor's degree in information technology and got a job with a Pune-based IT company. He worked hard and was soon a team leader.

Meanwhile, along with his job, Manish also completed his master's in computer application. Given his exceptional performance, the company sent him to the UK to work with a client directly. Earning in Pounds Sterling helped Manish improve the family's financial situation. He got a chance to follow his passion for cricket, becoming part of a cricket league club in the UK, and receiving many accolades for his performances. He once again considered fulfilling his dream of playing cricket professionally, but this time, he was too old. His inability to follow his passion was one of the reasons Manish was adamant that Kabita would have her chance and be supported on her journey.

Being a senior functionary in his company, Manish too, has a hectic schedule. However, he makes sure the kids get proper attention when Kabita is busy. He looks after them when he returns from the office, and when Kabita is working on recordings, Manish takes the kids out so she is undisturbed. When Kabita works late at night, Manish sits with her and responds to comments on her previous videos, capturing viewer suggestions and requests. Most days the two of them work till 11.30 p.m.

One cannot experience success without a little taste of failure. Like everyone else, Kabita too, has had her share of ups and downs. But Manish has always been there to support her. Kabita once received a very abusive comment for her recipe. She got emotional and planned to delete her channel. It was Manish who made her realise that negative and offensive comments are part of an influencer's journey. He also pointed out that 98 per cent of the comments she received were positive, so she should be happy about that rather than crying over a few negative comments.

Manish not only motivates Kabita but also guides her whenever he sees her going off track. When her channel achieved 1 million subscribers, Kabita felt that viewers would like whatever she cooked. Manish warned her, saying the kind of recipes that worked with a subscriber base of 1,000 or 10,000 would not work with 1 million. He suggested she be innovative. Kabita, however, ignored this wise advice and began sharing basic recipes on her channel. Suddenly, her subscriber growth and user engagement stagnated. Realising her mistake, Kabita quickly corrected herself and came up with many innovative videos, such as 'Six Series'. In this series, she shared six quick recipes in every video, such as six types of cold coffee, six types of rice, six types of tea and so on. She came up with many other innovative ideas and gradually regained her subscriber growth rate.

Besides being supportive, Manish is also creative. He comes up with out-of-the-box brand association ideas and amazing titles for the videos. For instance, during the COVID-19 lockdown, Kabita's video 'Instant jalebi for the whole family with just four spoons of maida' received more than 11 million views. 'Manish suggested the title,' says Kabita, 'and the words "4 spoons" made people curious. They wanted to see how it could be done.'

Although Kabita is famous for her recipes, her favourite dish is the chicken dum biryani prepared by Manish. She says, 'This journey would not have been possible without the encouragement and support of Manish. He is not only my husband, but also my mentor.'

IN CONCLUSION

Being a woman with professional aspirations is never easy. A large number of women are unable to build a career due to a lack of education. Even among educated women, the chances are that raising children and managing their home ends their professional careers. This is a sad reality.

However, digital media is a ray of hope for women. Kabita's journey showcases that by leveraging the power of digital media, a woman can create an admirable brand even from her home kitchen and share her art (recipes) with people across the world, while simultaneously taking care of her family responsibilities.

In the grand climax of the film *Ratatouille*, the food critic Anton Ego says, 'Not everyone can be a great artist, but a great artist can come from anywhere.' In today's world, these words have a lot of relevance. Because of the power of digital media, 'a great artist can come from anywhere'.

Perspectives from Kabita Singh

- When you are trying to create a brand, do not just partner with people who *want* to work with you. Partner with people who *believe* in you.
- If you are passionate about something and know the end goal, you will find ways, people and resources to help you. Don't deviate from your path for short-term gains.
- Don't think of money when you start. If you are passionate about your work and care for your viewers, the money will follow.
- Create high-quality and differentiated content.
- Always focus on viewers; don't compromise their trust for brand deals. You are relevant for brands because you are relevant to viewers.

NIKUNJ LOTIA

NIKUNJ LOTIA

From Bartender to Comedy Superstar

You have to believe in yourself, that's the secret.

—Charlie Chaplin

People often think that comedians who make them laugh on stage must have been born with the wonderful gift of a humorous life. But that is not the case at all. In reality, the backstories of many comedians are both painful and sad. It seems contradictory, but it is true. A case in point is Nikunj Lotia, popularly known as 'Be YouNick', a leading personality in the world of comedy.

But do you know what he faced growing up?

While other children attended class, he would stand outside the classoom because his parents had not been able to pay the school fees on time. For years, he slept on railway platforms. When he started his YouTube journey, people laughed at him. But he was never one to give up so easily. Despite his troubles and sadness, Nikunj (Nick) had an innate talent—to make other people laugh. It was what took him from the streets of Dombivli, a Mumbai suburb, to the glamorous world of Los Angeles, the entertainment capital of the world.

By April 2024, more than 9 million people were following Nick across digital platforms. He was the only digital creator from India at VidCon 2019, the annual summit of social media stars, in California. He has collaborated with both international and Indian celebrities, including Ayushmann Khurrana, Alia Bhatt, Boman Irani, Madhuri Dixit, Varun Dhawan and Rajkummar Rao. But Nick's achievements do not end there. Beyond being a celebrity in the digital world, he has a stake in six other businesses, including two food trucks in the US. He co-created the viral hip-hop rap song, 'Ala Motha Shana'. Nick is also one of the most preferred creators for collaborations by brands like Tinder, OPPO, William Lawson's, KIA Motors, Gillette, Beardo, etc. In 2021, BeYouNick collaborated with upGrad to release the web series *The Office Canteen*, which won the Best Collaboration Award at the inaugural YouTube Works Award India.

Are you wondering how a person from such a challenging background reached such extraordinary heights? Well, you will find the answers in the incredible story below.

THE BEGINNING

Nick was born on 9 November 1989, into a wealthy Gujarati family. His father owned a couple of shops, residential properties in Colaba, one of Mumbai's posh localities, as well as a farmhouse outside Mumbai. When Nick was just two years old, his father's business collapsed. Circumstances compelled the family to sell the flats, shut the shops and settle in Dombivli, a small middle-class suburb.

With no income, the family lived on their savings, but it was never enough. Soon, paying even the school fees became a challenge for Nick's parents, and his elder brother, Punit Lotia, had to drop out of school. To ensure this did not happen to Nick, his mother, Veena Lotia, began making *theplas*, a popular Gujarati flatbread made with fenugreek, which his brother delivered to local shops. Nick was too young to help then, but as he grew older, he took a part-time job at a cyber café.

He went to college on a student loan. 'I studied hotel management at Sir J.J. School of Art, which was in Mumbai's Chhatrapati Shivaji Terminus (CST) area, 50 kilometres from my home in Dombivli. To specialise in bartending, I would take evening classes at Khar, about 15 kilometres from CST. To repay my loan and support the family, I worked at night as a bartender, earning ₹350 a shift,' Nick remembers. By the time his late-night work finished, the last local train had left. So he would sleep on railway platforms. Early the next morning, he would take the first local train home. Strangely, he began to enjoy the struggle.

Having completed his education, Nick went to Goa to work as a bartender and wedding planner. He was there for almost a year. When he returned to Mumbai, he had no job, and the financial condition at home was dire. So Nick took up a job at a call centre. He says, 'I hated that job, but I stuck around for three years because it paid well.'

At the call centre, a colleague showed Nick some comedy videos on YouTube. Nick had been the class clown in his schooldays. Seeing the videos, he thought of creating similar comedy videos to share with his friends. In 2013, he started a YouTube channel, *Not so funny*. It did not take off. In 2014, Nick started a new channel, *Be YouNick*. One night, he uploaded a video about how guys make fools of themselves to impress women. Anxiously, he waited to see the response. For hours, nothing happened. Staring at the screen, Nick fell asleep.

When he woke the next morning, the video had received around 2,000 views. Surprisingly, the number of views on this one video on *Be YouNick* was more than the cumulative views of eight videos on *Not so funny*. Nick looked at the number in surprise, rubbing his eyes. Unknowingly, something had worked. And an inspiring journey was about to begin.

There are many valuable lessons to be learnt from the evolution of Be YouNick as a personal brand. A few of them are shared here.

CULTIVATE SELF-BELIEF EARLY IN LIFE

Self-belief is the most critical quality in being successful in life. Maybe that's why 'believe in yourself' is the most common advice people receive when they approach successful people for guidance. A person's childhood experiences and environment also play a prominent role in developing self-belief. Growing up in a hostile or unhappy environment can demolish a person's confidence and belief in themselves.

Nick's childhood was difficult at every point. Paying school fees on time was always a challenge. There were times he was made to stand out of class for 8 hours because of this. He says, 'I remember being asked to leave school in front of all my classmates. It was a very embarrassing situation.' It was particularly terrible for a child who did not understand the larger picture. Sadly, this kind of emotional abuse tore down Nick's self-belief.

In every classroom, there is a category of students infamous as the backbenchers. They are often considered time-wasters who score low marks, and teachers usually shout at them. Nick recalls, 'I was always an average student, so my place in class was as a backbencher.' When people make you feel you are not good enough, you can easily lose confidence in yourself. The continuous taunting about being a backbencher made Nick feel unworthy of any aspirational goals.

Feeling helpless and vulnerable, uncertain about what the future held, Nick was deeply disturbed emotionally. But even in the most negative of circumstances, small positive actions can make a big difference. Being spiritual, Nick used to visit Ram Mandir, a temple near his house. Praying to God and touching his head on the Om painted on the wall, was a source of positive strength for him. He also started to watch motivational videos by American speakers like Eric Thomas. Gradually, he began noticing some exciting changes in his own thought process. He began loving himself and decided to change his situation.

In those days, Govinda was the top comedy star in Bollywood. His funny dialogues made Nick laugh, and he gradually realised the power of humour. He decided to pull the humour from anything that happened around him. One of the most difficult things about being a comedian is that one has to be original all the time. So Nick started thinking of multiple funny answers for every question, insult and humiliation he had faced. Comedy became an escape for him, allowing him to enjoy the situation he was in without losing himself. A newly developed sense of humour also helped Nick make a place for himself among his classmates. The children laughed at his jokes and enjoyed his company. Over time, Nick developed a sense of what was likely going on in other peoples' minds, and what they would find amusing in different situations. The attention Nick began to get because of his jokes helped to bolster his self-esteem. Within a short period, Nick had become famous as the class clown.

Now, Nick says, 'People think I am spontaneous, but my reactions to situations come from the fifteen or twenty years of fighting bullies and giving it back. I spent years perfecting this ability. My hard phase shaped my perspective, and my sense of humor and storytelling skills probably came from that.'

FIND A NICHE, AND BECOME MASTER OF IT

The word 'niche' can mean different things to different people, but generally, it means a specific area. Being willing to focus on something niche can result in massive returns. People always prefer working with an expert, and there is less direct competition in a niche. Moreover, choosing a niche elevates your chances of creating a unique brand.

Within the restaurant industry, bartending is considered niche. It is an extremely social profession, as it requires a person to be creative while putting them at the centre. A bartender specialises in making a wide variety of drinks. He creates a fun experience for guests and dazzles them with bar gymnastics such as throwing and catching ice cubes in glasses, spinning and flipping multiple bottles and so on. All of this is done to rock 'n' roll music. That said, becoming a bartender is not easy. It is a physically and psychologically demanding profession, and it takes years of practice to become a celebrated bartender.

When Nick was eighteen years old, he saw the movie *Cocktail*, in which Hollywood superstar Tom Cruise played a bartender. His charisma and the glamour of bartending, as shown in the movie, inspired Nick to become a bartender. He arranged a loan and took admission in a hotel management course and to specialise in bartending, he joined evening classes at Cocktails & Dreams, a bartending school in Khar. Though Nick enjoyed his courses, he worried about how to arrange the next fee installment. Amidst this uncertainty, an opportunity emerged.

The bartender who was to represent Cocktails & Dreams at an event in Pune did not turn up on the day of the event. The owner of the academy asked Nick if he would step in. Nick replied with a smile, 'If I get some money, I will.' He got ₹350. But customer feedback about Nick was very positive, and going forward, he began getting bartending opportunities as a freelancer. The money thus earned helped Nick to pay his fees and pay off his loan.

By the end of the course, Nick was an expert. At one bartending competition he created a cocktail that was loved by the judges. When they asked him the ingredients, he said, 'The way vodka is a popular alcoholic beverage in Russia and tequila is popular in Mexico, *desi daru* is a popular alcoholic beverage in India. I have used *desi daru* in the cocktail.' Everyone laughed at this humorous answer, and appreciated Nick's creativity. He won the competition.

Goa has long been world-famous for its party places and nightclubs. Having completed his education and training in Mumbai, Nick decided to move to Goa to explore opportunities there. While in Goa, he worked as a bartender at night and as a wedding planner by day. The life in Goa was good, but Nick's parents wanted him back home. When Nick returned to Mumbai a year later, he had no job. The clubs and restaurants where he had previously worked had new talent in place. After struggling for a few months, Nick decided to take a job at a call centre. 'I missed my bartending days and was not enjoying the call centre much. But I was getting ₹20,000 per month as salary, and I needed that to support my family,' he recalls.

While working at the call centre, Nick got to know about a YouTube channel called *Life According to Jimmy*. Jimmy Tatro, an American film-maker and comedian, mixed sketch comedy with his own spin on everyday life. This channel nurtured Nick's fascination for sketch comedy. Nick recalled the days of being the school comic and thought of creating his own YouTube channel. In 2013, he started *Not so funny*. Nick says, 'This channel was exactly what its name said. No one watched my videos and colleagues made fun of me.'

One evening, Nick was sharing his frustration with one of his friends. During their discussion, possible reasons for the channel not having worked surfaced. Nick said to his friend, 'I want to create a popular channel like *Life According to Jimmy*. It's my dream.' His friend replied, 'The channel name could be *Life According to Nick*.' But Nick shook his head in denial and said, 'I don't want to be a copycat. I want to be unique.' His friend responded with the suggestion that the channel name could be *Be YouNick*. 'It's a play on 'be unique' and has the name Nick too,' he said. Nick liked the idea very much. At the time, neither knew that one day, *Be YouNick* would surpass *Life According to Jimmy* in the number of subscribers.

PRIORITISE LONG-TERM GOALS OVER SHORT-TERM GAIN

We live in a society that thrives on instant gratification. We feel low if our friends don't like our social media posts, if our pizza is not delivered in 30 minutes, or if someone doesn't give us a smile. When it comes to achieving any worthwhile goal, anxiety has to be controlled, and instant gratification avoided. Long-term goals take significant time, effort and planning to achieve.

Nick says, 'You can only reach your long-term goal by regularly taking small steps. My call centre job was giving me short-term gain in the form of a monthly salary. But it was taking away the time required for my heart's calling, to become a sketch comedian.' After three years at the call centre, Nick received a bonus amount equivalent to two months' salary. He decided to put the amount towards the family expenses while directing all his focus towards his YouTube channel. So he quit the job. His parents said nothing but a relative told him, 'I can give you in writing that you will fail in whatever you are planning to do.' But Nick wanted to focus on his goal. There was no Plan B.

Within two months, the bonus money was gone and there was no revenue from the YouTube channel. Nick was in desperate straits. At the time, Ramesh Raut, owner of The Raut's Family Salon in Dombivli, offered him financial help. Within a month, the borrowed money too, was gone. Ramesh offered further assistance but Nick was not comfortable taking such large favours from a good friend. So he decided to take up another call centre job. And though he did so, his mind remained on video ideas. He found the job so suffocating that he left within the hour on day one. Nick says, 'I quit my job and swore never to work for anyone else again.'

But dreams were one thing, the realities of life another. The challenge was the money required for survival. Nick says, 'I could have survived on *vada pavs* (a local street food), but I needed money to buy groceries for home.' As if some higher power had heard, his phone rang. An old contact was calling to tell Nick about a bartender vacancy at a club near CST, in Mumbai's Fort area. Nick thought he could focus on his YouTube channel during the day and work at the bar at night, so he said yes.

And so he funded his YouTube channel for a substantial period with his part-time bartending job, which finished at about 2 a.m. By then, the last train from CST to Dombivli had left, and cab to Dombivli would have cost about ₹2,000. Nick was making only ₹350 per shift, so the cab option was ruled out. Nick had no option but to sleep on a station bench. He says ruefully, 'Benches in the railway platforms became my friends. I did not care anymore. It had been my choice to leave my job and pursue my passion. I had the belief that all this would lead to something.'

In 2015, during the ICC Cricket World Cup, Star Sports launched the ad campaign *Mauka Mauka*, which became a huge hit. Fans created many spoofs and versions of the ad, and it was the most trending topic throughout the tournament. Meanwhile, an exciting video was released on *Be YouNick*. In no time, the video went viral and achieved close to a million views. Nick says, 'This was my fifteenth video. The previous fourteen had achieved a few thousand views at most.' The video made Nick so famous that people began calling him the *mauka mauka wala ladka* (the boy from *mauka mauka*). His friends suggested he make more videos around the same theme, but Nick did not want to be known for this one theme. He wanted to be known as Nick. He told his friends, 'I am here to make sketch comedy, not just *mauka mauka* videos.' Nick created forty more videos on various themes, but none was as popular as the *mauka mauka* one. Nevertheless, Nick remained focused on achieving his long-term goal.

Meanwhile, a famous content company offered Nick a job with a monthly salary of ₹50,000. Nick thought over it, wondering that if he used his creativity to write for them, what would he write for himself? He did not wish to dilute his focus. So he politely declined. In time, *Be YouNick*'s videos such as 'Once upon a time in Dombivli', 'First Date', 'Men will be Men' and a few others became very popular, enhancing Nick's credibility in the genre of subtle comedy. Slowly, his audience grew.

Nick says, 'Don't think of monetisation when you start out. If I had, I would have become restless after five videos and would never have made another forty-five.' By 2016, *Be YouNick* had become a popular YouTube channel, and people had started recognising Nick. 'At the bar, many customers would approach me for selfies with them. Sometimes, on a train, youngsters would ask for selfies. It was an honour.'

But, while fame had come, the money was still slow. When his channel reached 500,000 subscribers, a biker t-shirt brand approached Nick for placement in a video. Nick asked for ₹2 lakhs, but got only ₹8,000. By the time *Be YouNick* achieved 1 million subscribers, other brands started approaching Nick for collaborations. Then came the viral video, 'Job interview gone wrong', with Bollywood actor Rajkummar Rao. It took Nick's popularity to the next level.

Over time, Nick has become a preferred collaborator for many renowned brands. He says, 'It's a good feeling. Earlier, I accepted any brand deal that was offered to me, at any amount. Now I'm in a position to pick and choose. But one thing remains constant between the past and the present—I have never compromised on my ethics. I research a brand thoroughly before getting associated. Then I review the fitment of the brand in my script. If everything goes well, I collaborate.'

Now, Nick is a full-time content creator who can afford to live life on his own terms. But what really makes him happy is giving his family everything they deserve. Once, he bought a pair of gold earrings for his grandmother. Seeing how happy the gift made her was the best feeling in the world for him. There was a time when Nick would avoid partying with his friends because he didn't have money to pay his share. But now, he makes sure he pays for his friends. 'It was my dream to pay the bills of my friends without thinking twice. And so I pay wherever we party, be it in India, Amsterdam, New York, Los Angeles or anywhere else.' Recently, he bought a house for his family. His sacrifice in the short term has given him substantial gains in the long term.

WHEN YOU DON'T HAVE RESOURCES, BECOME RESOURCEFUL

Sketch comedy consists of a series of short scenes called 'sketches', which are usually a few minutes in length. For those who grew up in the 1980s and 1990s, Jaspal Bhatti's *Flop Show* on Doordarshan was their first experience of sketch comedy. Usually, a group of comic actors perform such sketches.

As Nick was focused on sketch comedy, he required locations for shoots and team members to act along with him. But he did not have the money to rent locations or hire professional comic actors. Nick says, 'Dombivli is full of kind and helpful people. When I asked people to allow me to shoot at restaurants, shops and even the police station gate, they allowed me to do so without charging anything. Getting a live location saved a lot of cost. Had I been in Andheri or Goregaon, I would have been asked to pay for setup and studios.' When Nick needed an office, Ramesh Raut offered a section at his salon. Nick laughs, 'I still do some of my meetings at Ramesh's salon.' As the popularity of *Be YouNick* has grown, the popularity of the places shown in the videos have grown as well. *Be YouNick* has popularised Dombivli as the 'Republic of Dombivli', a name that has caught on with the audience.

Returning to the challenges of Nick's early days, getting people to act with him was a big problem. He requested many people to act along with him and met numerous videographers to shoot his videos. Most of them ignored Nick. A few said yes, but didn't turn up. Those who did left after one or two videos. Nick says ruefully, 'Perhaps they didn't see a future in working with me.' As a workaround, Nick explored opportunities with the students of Whistling Woods International, a film school in Mumbai. A few of the students came forward to help him.

It took Nick more than a year to get his team together. The first person to join was Murali. One day, Nick went to meet a videographer accompanied by a person named Murali, who was not interested in continuing his studies and was looking to do something creative. That videographer never met Nick again, but Murali liked Nick's ideas. He came forward to join *Be YouNick*. While playing cricket, another boy called Sushant asked Nick, 'Bro, next video *kab upload hoga*?' ('When will the next video be uploaded?'). Nick was surprised to know that someone watched his videos. In trying to learn more about Sushant, he got to know that Sushant was a video editor. When Nick asked him to help with editing his videos, Sushant happily agreed.

At a wedding he attended, Nick coincidentally met Vivek, a cinematographer. They had dinner together and became friends. During the conversation, Vivek told Nick that he was getting bored doing monotonous wedding shoots and wanted to do something creative and challenging. Nick said, 'If you want to do something creative, why don't you join *Be YouNick*?' Nick showed Vivek a few videos on his mobile phone. Vivek liked the concepts and agreed to join Nick on his journey.

Nick met Tushar at a gym. He was a mechanical engineer who had left his dull engineering job in Dubai and was trying to figure out what to do next. Nick felt Tushar had natural acting talent and convinced him to join his team.

When the business started growing, Nick wanted someone to manage finances and the back office. He posted an intern requirement on Facebook. Only one person, a youngster named Anant, turned up. *Be YouNick* has grown a lot over time, and Anant has evolved from an intern into the finance head.

For a long time, Nick tried to get his school friend Omkar on board. He thought Omkar's sense of humour was great and would be a solid asset. When Omkar saw that *Be YouNick* was getting some traction, he was finally convinced. Nick makes the concepts, and Omkar helps the team with script and dialogue writing. Today, Nick says, 'Many other people came and went, but these few have remained with me for years.'

Writing relatable and family-friendly comedy content is extremely difficult because there needs to be an element of uniqueness and originality for a joke to work. Nick explains how he works, 'I just look around. Interesting observations come from everywhere. When I have a thought, or I see a funny situation, I save it.' The team adds head, tail and unique twists to the observations, flesh them out into proper sketches, and then execute them. The channel's satire is easy to understand, incisive and clean. Nick has never felt the need to use dirty or abusive language to make people laugh or attract attention.

Making videos is one challenge, getting them noticed is another. Initially, Nick had thought his 2,000 friends on Facebook would naturally subscribe to his channel. He was wrong. When they did not, he started a push strategy. He sent messages to all his friends. Nick says, 'If you check the messages of people who were my friends back then, you will find links to my first video everywhere.' He also spammed Facebook pages of popular forums like BuzzFeed, ScoopWhoop, Rajnikanth v/s CID Jokes, and others. Ever the stalwart supporter, Nick's friend Ramesh Raut, would also spread the word, asking all his salon customers to subscribe to *Be YouNick*. Many people liked the videos and shared them further. In time, the subscriber base started increasing from hundreds to thousands to millions. Nick says today, 'Honestly, I'm here because of the hustle, and that's the best advice I can give—keep hustling. The universe loves a stubborn heart!'

STAY CONSISTENT, STAY HUMBLE

When we ask people what they consider traits of successful people, the typical answers are intelligence, ambition, perseverance, luck, etc. Indeed, all these factors matter. But two other aspects should be highlighted instead of being hidden within. These are consistency and humility.

According to Nick, mastering anything in life takes consistent practice every day. He thinks that artists should consistently improve their creative style, use new tools and features and keep looking for new ways to engage with their audiences. He himself works 16 hours a day. Whatever the ups and downs of life, Nick has never stopped making videos. Every day, he posts content on Instagram, and every week he uploads a video on YouTube and Facebook. Often, people who discover him on one platform also follow him on another.

Usually, when people fail to get immediate results from their actions, they discontinue the practice. However, results do not come quickly in life. They come from making incremental progress and improvements over an extended period. One of Nick's strongest qualities is that he does not give up when his ideas are not working out. He says, 'Being a content creator is not easy. Like any other career, massive hard work is involved in content creation. You can never rely on making one fantastic piece that will go viral. However, if you are consistent and bring out many good pieces of content, you will increase your followers and engagement.'

When Nick is not working on ideas, he is looking out for them. To share an incident, Nick was once invited to the US to participate in a conference about promoting US tourism in India. After the conference, he stayed at the venue and tried to understand what the other participants did in life. Interestingly, he met a Maharashtrian chef, who was toying with the idea of starting an Indian food truck in the US. While talking to him, Nick saw a niche opportunity in selling Maharashtrian fast food. He liked the chef as a person and decided to invest. The outcome was the Feast India Company, a food truck brand that sells Maharashtrian fast food such as *vada pav*, *missal pav*, *chai* and *chaas* in San Francisco, six days a week. Nick says enthusiastically, 'It's a big hit!' Seeing Feast India Company's success, Nick invested in One Bite Stand, another food truck brand in the US. Similarly, by meeting people and talking about their ideas, he has invested in many other ventures.

Nick travels worldwide and collaborates with some of the biggest names, but he still lives in Dombivli, plays football with the same old friends and eats *vada pav* at the same streetside stall. He says, 'Success has come to me after a long struggle, and I don't want it to get to my head. The best part about this place is that people here still treat me as the same old Nick who had nothing. That keeps me grounded.' Nick has learnt many essential lessons about humility from successful celebrities. He once met Tom Hanks, one of Hollywood's biggest superstars, and was amazed by the man's humility and simplicity. Nick says, 'Success doesn't have a fixed formula. One can either get it by hard work or by luck. But failure has a pattern—having a big ego and surrounding yourself with yes men. Always be humble.'

IN CONCLUSION

Nick's journey is truly remarkable. Beyond becoming a celebrity, creating many businesses and changing the financial situation of his family, Nick has made a positive difference in the lives of millions of people. Using the power of laughter, he has made millions of people laugh and feel good amidst their gloom. By writing the unique script of his life, he has brought lightness and hope to millions of children from underprivileged backgrounds or who do not wish to follow conventional career paths.

Nick says he has just started. Every morning, he wakes up with a thought to create something new. It will be truly inspirational to watch his creations and dreams evolve and leave their positive imprint on society.

Perspectives from Nick

- Don't compare yourself to others. Focus on your strength and craft. Be unique!
- Do what you love to do so that you don't get stressed out when things are not working.
- There is a lot of competition in every industry. To stand out in your field, you have to take risks, come up with fresh and innovative ideas and develop a thick skin.
- Life is not a sprint. It's a marathon. Keep big goals in life and work on them every day. Towards the end of the week, you would have progressed.
- Many people do something to become famous. I suggest you stick to what you love doing, with a lot of commitment, and you will have your audience.

PRAJAKTA KOLI

PRAJAKTA KOLI

From Radio Intern to Comedy Queen

Instead of letting your hardships and failures discourage or exhaust you, let them inspire you. Let them make you even hungrier to succeed.

—Michelle Obama

In the dictionary, the word 'failure' comes before the word 'success'. Similarly in life, failure usually precedes success. Here are a few examples. Oprah Winfrey was fired from her first television anchor job. She ended up creating one of the highest-rated television talk shows in the world. Michael Jordan was rejected from his eighth-grade basketball team. He ended up becoming the greatest basketball player of all time. Walt Disney was fired from a newspaper because he was not creative enough. He ended up creating the largest entertainment empire in the world. Steven Spielberg was rejected three times by a film school. He ended up becoming one of the wealthiest film-makers in the world. They all fell, but they picked themselves up again and created history. This is a similar story.

By the age of eleven, Prajakta Koli had decided on her career plan. She wished to become India's top radio jockey (RJ). She spent hours listening to FM channels and participating in extra-curricular activities aligned to her career goal. As a first step towards her dream, she started working as an intern at a radio station. However, the internship went nowhere. A year later, she got the opportunity to host her first radio show. It was a miserable failure. Her self-confidence took a beating. From loving radio, she began to hate it. Eventually, at the start of 2015, she quit her RJ career.

In February of the same year, Prajakta began her new journey as a YouTuber. Today, she is India's top female comedy YouTuber. As of April 2024, she has 7.1 million subscribers on YouTube, 7.9 million followers on Instagram and 1.2 million on Facebook. Her popularity brought her collaborations with celebrities like Hrithik Roshan, Ayushmann Khurrana, Kajol, Nawazuddin Siddiqui and Badshah. She has also acted in the short film, *Khayali Pulao*, the Netflix series *Mismatched*, and the Karan Johar produced film *Jug Jugg Jeeyo*. Prajakta has also made a few music videos like *Shameless* (2017), *No Offence* (2018), and *Yeh Diss Gaana Hain* (2020). She has also collaborated with Michelle Obama (former US First Lady), on a YouTube original documentary on the education of girls.

Prajakta has many other achievements to her credit. She was the first YouTuber in the world to interview YouTube's Global CEO, Susan Wojcicki. She is also the only one from India to have been invited by Marvel Comics to collaborate with the cast of the American superhero film *Captain Marvel*. In February 2019, she was included in the *Forbes* list of 30 under 30 and *Entrepreneur India*'s 35 under 35. In the same year, she was featured in *Outlook Business Magazine*'s list of Women of Worth and received *Cosmopolitan*'s YouTuber of the Year award. In 2020, Prajakta was featured on the cover of *BW Businessworld* in one of their lists of Most Influential Women.

In 2022, Prajakta was appointed by UNDP (United Nations Development Programme) as India's first Youth Climate Champion. In January 2023, she attended the World Economic Forum held in Davos as one of the six content creators invited globally for the event. Prajakta participated in discussions centered around critical themes such as climate action, social justice and global healthcare. In 2024, she was awarded Climate Influencer of the Year at the NDTV Indian of the Year event held in New Delhi.

This then is the story of Prajakta Koli, failed radio intern who became one of the most popular and loved creators in India.

THE BEGINNING

Prajakta Koli was born on 27 June 1993, in Thane, a Mumbai suburb. Her mother, Archana Koli, worked as a school teacher, while her father, Manoj Koli, ran a restaurant. She did her schooling at Vasant Vihar High School, Thane, and earned a bachelor's degree in mass media from V.G. Vaze College of Arts, Science and Commerce, Mulund, another Mumbai suburb.

From childhood, Prajakta spent hours listening to FM radio. While her family would wait for songs, she would wait for the warm and friendly voice of the RJs. In those days, being an RJ. was not a popular profession. But she enjoyed listening to them so much that in Class VI, she decided she wanted to be an RJ. Prajakta always believed in having a plan and sticking to it. An average student, she never missed an opportunity to participate in public speaking competitions. At morning assemblies in school, she was the teachers' preferred choice to read the news and lead the pledge. In college, she got involved in theatre and anchoring.

After graduation, she joined a radio channel as an intern and eventually hosted a show. However, things weren't as pleasant as she had expected. The show flopped. A chorus of self-doubt began filling her head. While contemplating what to do next, she was spotted by Sudeep Lahiri from One Digital Entertainment, who suggested she start making content on YouTube. Back then, YouTube as a career choice was unheard of. Hence, Prajakta ignored Sudeep's advice for a few months. However, as her radio career continued to fail, she thought of giving the YouTube idea a shot. On 12 February 2015, Prajakta posted her first video. She never looked back.

There are many valuable lessons to be gleaned from the evolution of Prajakta Koli as a personal brand. A few are shared here.

RESTORE YOUR FAITH IN YOURSELF

Imagine believing you can do something very well for nearly a decade. Not only thinking so, but putting in every effort to become the best in your chosen field. But then a day comes when you fail in your chosen career, and that too, publicly. How would you feel? Perhaps you would lose faith in yourself? This is what happened to Prajakta.

As a young girl, Prajakta filled pages with autographs by and to herself. Her parents realised very early that she was more inclined towards the arts than academics. Perhaps, that's why they never gave too much attention to her report card. Instead, they pushed her to try new things such as dance, theatre and debate. They applauded her even when she got just a certificate of participation. Her father would say, 'Prajakta, don't be average. Either be below average or above average.' Growing up, Prajakta did not really understand his words, but today she knows their beauty. They helped her grow to be a confident person.

The more you practise speaking in front of others, the better you become. In school, Prajakta was active in any activity that required speaking in front of others. At home, she repeatedly recorded voice samples in her mother's voice recorder. Before her final year undergraduate exams, Prajakta prepared a list of all the radio stations in Mumbai. She spent nights and weekends preparing CDs of her voice recordings, assembling photocopies of her certificates and collecting recommendations from people with whom she had worked. She prepared separate packets for every radio station and went with her parents to drop them at the various stations. Eventually, she was accepted as an intern at Fever 104 FM. Prajakta was thrilled to begin her dream journey and celebrated with her parents.

But her glorified vision of radio was soon shattered. Instead of becoming an RJ, she found herself working in the production team on 14-hour shifts. Also, she found it difficult to adjust to the culture of the radio station. She started to feel she was not talented enough for radio. As much as she had once loved the idea, now she began hating her job. Going to work felt like a battle with herself. She continued, reminding herself this was just the start.

Finally, after a year-long internship, Prajakta's manager told her there was an opening for an RJ on the late-night show, *Call Centre*. Though the show's timings were odd—midnight to 2 a.m., it was finally the opportunity she had been waiting for to be on air. So Prajakta grabbed it. She enjoyed recording the show, but the audience was not responsive. In the second week, she was told not to do the show live, but pre-record her sessions. The opportunity that had looked interesting initially suddenly became boring. Imagine sitting in a room alone, not being able to speak to anyone. She felt she was doing a fake show and her motivation level went down. The show flopped, and Prajakta's self-confidence took a beating. She decided a career as radio jokey was not for her. Her longtime dream of becoming India's best RJ had crashed, and she felt devastated.

What happened to Prajakta can happen to any of us. When faced with failure, it is challenging to convince ourselves to move ahead. A setback in our dream career can often appear to be the end of the road. But it is well to remember the old saying: when one door closes, another opens. Instead of staring in regret at the closed door, one should look for the new door opening up somewhere. Prajakta's parents consoled her saying, 'You are a star, with unique talents. Maybe there is a better and brighter career waiting for you.' Prajakta slowly restored her faith in herself and started looking for another opportunity. When she decided to be a YouTuber, she looked into the mirror and encouraged herself, saying, 'YouTube is going to be my new start.'

ALWAYS BE READY FOR SURPRISES

Carl Sandburg, a famous American writer and winner of three Pulitzer Prizes, once said, 'Nearly all the best things that came to me in life have been unexpected, unplanned by me.' When we plan too much, we usually look for perfect conditions. But things rarely fall into perfect place. Sometimes, the thrill of trying something new, a positive attitude and self-confidence can bring surprises that can change your life. Something similar happened to Prajakta when she seized the opportunity to meet Hrithik Roshan.

From his debut film *Kaho Naa Pyaar Hai*, Hrithik Roshan conquered millions of hearts, and Prajakta's was one of them.

When Prajakta heard that Hrithik would be coming to the radio station to promote the film *Bang Bang*, she expressed her desire to meet him, much to the derisive laughter of her co-workers, who scoffed she would not be allowed to come within ten feet of him. However, when Hrithik arrived at the radio station, Prajakta could not stop herself. She says, 'I thought, he is standing in front of me, let me take a picture! I'll think about my job later.' Using her elbows to make her way through the crowd, she eventually reached Hrithik and said, 'Hey! Can I get a picture with you?' She shot a video in which they both say, 'Oh my God!' But Prajakta was delighted with her fan moment and posted the video on Instagram.

That day, Sudeep Lahiri, Vice President at One Digital Entertainment, India's leading digital video and creator network, was also present at the studio. Impressed by Prajakta's bubbling energy, he asked her to start a YouTube channel. To talk about this, he invited her to his office. Prajakta did not think YouTube was a career option, so she felt that meeting Sudeep would be a waste of time. But Sudeep always stopped to say hello to Prajakta whenever he happened to visit the radio station. With her radio career failing, Prajakta was not sure what to do next. In limbo, she decided to meet Sudeep. Three months later, she went, thinking that if she cracked the interview, she would be a YouTuber.

When she met Sudeep, she told him upfront that music-, fashion- and beauty-related topics were not her cup of tea. In those days, Prajakta wrote a humorous blog, which only four people, including her parents, read. She showed it to Sudeep. He suggested she would be a better fit in comedy and offered to help her create something in the comedy space. When the meeting ended, she asked him if she had got the job. Sudeep was astonished at how clueless Prajakta was. He smiled and told her, 'My team and I will be working for you, not the other way round.' It was Prajakta's turn to be astonished.

She was scared about this new journey, but her parents encouraged her not to worry about anything and give herself two years to achieve results. She did not want the channel to have her name, but a smart title. The first one that came to mind was, *MostlySane*. To convince her team at One Digital Entertainment, Prajakta explained that she was going to make sense, but she would also show herself getting away with doing stupid things. To her surprise, everyone hated the name. But as the channel was supposed to go live the very next day, and no one had a better suggestion, she went ahead with *MostlySane*.

When she started, Prajakta did not know how to make YouTube content. So she just took content ideas from multiple places and created a video. On 12 February 2015, she posted her first video '5 types of singles on Valentine's Day'. With Valentine's Day around the corner, the video earned over 1,000 views. Within the first four months, she had 2,000 subscribers, and soon had over 20,000 subscribers. Prajakta says, 'With YouTube, you get addicted to the number of views, likes and dislikes. It's an open and transparent platform, while being interactive.' She began to enjoy the process, and within two years, she gained over 500,000 subscribers on her YouTube channel.

To celebrate her birthday and meteoric rise on YouTube, Sudeep and Gurpreet Singh, COO and co-founder of One Digital Entertainment, arranged a surprise meeting for her with Hrithik Roshan. She was told to go to a bungalow in Juhu, where Hrithik surprised her by opening the door. He said, 'Hi Prajakta, how have you been?' Prajakta was shocked to discover that Hrithik even remembered her name. He invited her in and asked her to cut the chocolate cake he had arranged for her. She was delighted with this birthday surprise, and cried when it was time to bid Hrithik goodbye.

CREATE A BIGGER VISION FOR YOURSELF

Have you heard the famous story of breaking stones and building a monument? A woman was once walking down a street and noticed a group of labourers breaking stones. Intrigued, she went up to one of them and asked him what he was doing. The man replied abruptly, 'Can't you see? I am breaking stones.' She then asked the same question to the next man. To her surprise, he said, 'I am helping to build the world's tallest church.' Both labourers were doing the same work, but their vision was very different. The one with the larger vision was happier and more productive. In similar vein, by having a bigger vision of her work, Prajakta has made a mark in the crowded world of YouTube.

Growing up, Prajakta had enjoyed dancing and done many theatre shows, so she was not camera-shy. However, when she started her channel, she was rather insecure about herself. Her defence was to wear a lot of make-up and pick content ideas and delivery styles from other YouTubers. But she soon realised that she was best when she was authentic and not a copy of anyone else. Prajakta created a bigger vision for herself and decided to stand out based on her unique identity. She says, 'You can only go so far if you copy others. Your audience will know when you copy someone or use a fake accent. People like authenticity. You need to be "you". Slowly people will start to resonate with you if you connect with them on a regular basis.'

Within comedy, there are various niches. Prajakta was not a stand-up comedian who could crack jokes on the go. She describes her creative process as observational humour, which is exaggerating everyday situations in a funny manner. Prajakta's skits often portray a typical Indian middle-class family in daily life situations. For these skits, she created a fictional family with characters that include Archana (mother), Manoj (father) and Montu (younger brother). She plays all the characters herself, changing wigs and make-up. Prajakta says, 'Comments are a great way of taking feedback about your content and writing new content.' Funnily enough, the character of Montu gained so much popularity that the audience began asking for Montu videos. Over time, Prajakta has added many new characters to her fictional family.

Prajakta's greatest fear is losing her connection with her audience, so she tries very hard not to miss a video upload deadline. She says, 'There's a lot of other content on YouTube and it's easy to get lost in the crowd of videos if you do just one video in a while. I try to be consistent. If I tell my viewers I am going to upload a video on a specific day, then I have to do so.' When Prajakta started her channel, she would post videos every Thursday. Currently, she posts new content every Tuesday, Thursday and Saturday.

In 2018, Prajakta became the first female comedy creator in India to have 1 million subscribers. In the same year, she won the Viral Queen of the Year at the IWM Digital Awards. In a short span of six years, she has posted over 840 videos on her channel.

Along with comedy content, she also deals with social issues bothering young girls, such as body image issues and online bullying. Her alignment to these topics led to many opportunities she had never dreamed of. In 2018, Prajakta appeared in WhatsApp's first-ever TVC, which addressed the significance of not spreading fake news. In the same year, she was selected as the Indian ambassador for the YouTube's Creators for Change initiative, one of fifty YouTubers chosen worldwide. In 2019, the

Bill and Melinda Gates Foundation invited her to their annual Goalkeepers Summit. She was also the first Indian digital creator to participate in the UN General Assembly.

Prajakta says, 'I don't think I have achieved a lot. I have just started, and I am greedy. I feel grateful for opportunities. But I also I understand it's just the beginning.'

GIVE YOUR BEST TO YOUR CONTENT

In comparison to TV serials and movies, videos created by YouTubers are not well-produced and edited. Besides, they don't have many special effects and animations. Then why do people loyally watch YouTubers? The answer is because of the exciting content. Prajakta explains, 'Content is the only thing that works on YouTube. It makes people take time from their lives. It keeps getting them back on the channel of a creator.' Prajakta takes her content creation process very seriously. While creating great content was difficult initially, she always made sure not to miss a deadline.

Prajakta says, 'Every week is trial and error.' Because of the internet's reach, the audience can come from any city, town or village. So it is challenging to balance what a creator wants to create with what the audience wants to watch. Prajakta thus works with topics that are common across locations and situations. Every video on her channel comes from experience. She likes observing her surroundings. She also goes to social media channels like X to pick up trending topics. She always keeps a notebook and pen in her bag. Every day, she writes little notes to herself on things she feels would make for good video ideas.

In June 2015, she was at her maternal grandmother's home in Delhi. She was due to post a video on the coming Thursday, and was running out of ideas. She observed that Delhi people used many words that were almost unknown to people in Mumbai. So she made a video on '10 hilarious words Delhiites use'. The video took off and in two months, her subscriber count had increased from 3,000 to 30,000. Prajakta says, 'When I started my channel, I prayed to God to give me 40,000 subscribers.' So she had reached close to her original target.

The rise in digital content has made YouTube a crowded space. When there are so many creators, there are inevitably multiple videos on similar topics, which in turn has made content creation difficult. Prajakta thinks that more than new content, differentiation is about presenting content in a new way. She says, 'Since my content is observational, it's very personal.' She has never made a video on something she doesn't know about. Though she is not an engineer, for instance, she makes the time to meet and observe engineers to learn about their lives and work before making a video on the topic of engineering and engineers.

Although Prajakta is one of India's most popular content creators, it has not been a smooth ride to get to where she is today. She faced many highs and lows along the way. There was a time she hit content block and went on autopilot mode. She had got too comfortable and was not listening to what her followers were telling her. She began losing followers and was on the verge of shutting down her channel. Prajakta recalls, 'I got lazy, and maybe that's why my content became irrelevant.'

She was about to quit when magic happened. There was a script lying on her desk that she had written long before but never shot because it was too extensive. She thought of doing it before quitting. That video, 'Types of people on WhatsApp groups', went viral. With the success of this video, she realised that quitting was not an option. She began trying new things, brought in new characters and just kept going. Within a year, her subscriber base grew from 200,000 to 3 million. Prajakta cautions, 'There is no perfect formula. A creator has to keep experimenting and learning what their audience likes to watch.'

One of the key reasons behind Prajakta's success is her disciplined schedule of uploading videos on YouTube. There are some things that work only on YouTube, and content that works on other social media channels. So she also creates content for Instagram, Facebook and X. Her discipline has made her one of the most consistent creators. As a result, her fan base has grown enormously. She is devoted to her audience. 'Whatever I have achieved is because of my audience. I never take them for granted,' she says. She interacts directly with her audience online, answering questions asked in the comments section. She also makes sure she is giving her audience quality content. She says reflectively, 'It's not easy to always come up with fresh content that will become popular. I have made peace with the fact that not everything I publish will go viral.'

IT IS GOOD TO BE FEARFUL

Intel's former CEO Andy Grove, famously said, 'Success breeds complacency. Complacency breeds failure. Only the paranoid survive.' When someone becomes very popular, it is natural for them to become overconfident and take things for granted. However, if one remains paranoid, they keep striving for perfection. That is the credo Prajakta follows.

She says, 'Every time I do something out of my comfort zone, I have doubts whether I will be able to do it. But I want to feel that self-doubt. I never want to enter any field with the feeling of overconfidence. Self-doubt helps me navigate things better.' When she was cast as a seventeen-year-old schoolgirl in her first film, *Khayali Pulao*, she did not know how she would play the role. To understand the characteristics of a normal teenage girl from rural North India, she spent days in a village and took pronunciation lessons. Her deep preparation for the role translated into a lovable and realistic performance.

When she was cast in the Netflix web series *Mismatched*, she knew there would be more eyeballs on her and expectations would be higher. Moreover, she was playing a character she had not written. For the first few days of the shoot, it was tough to break away from the creator personality and go into actor mode. After every shot, she would ask the director, '*Kaisa tha*? (How was it?) Can I see it?' With time, she got comfortable and stopped over-analysing her acting. Because of her YouTube experience, facing the camera came easily to Prajakta, but working with Bollywood stars in *Jug Jugg Jeeyo* made her nervous. But this lasted only till she got on set and the director helped her understand the character she was playing. It made her realise that all actors were just artists once the cameras began to roll.

While grabbing new opportunities, Prajakta ensures her YouTube video schedule and audience engagement does not get affected. Besides, she performs at many on-site events such as college fests, YouTube FanFest and Comic Con. Sometimes, she has such a busy schedule that breakfast, lunch and dinner happen in different cities. Even with a super-busy schedule and all the work pressure, Prajakta continues to connect with her audience at a personal level.

Perhaps the question in your mind is, how does she manage it all? The answer is—thanks to the splendid team that supports her. Prajakta says, 'Earlier, I didn't like delegating. That was a mistake. The combined effort of multiple qualified minds is always better than one mind working on multiple things. My biggest strength is my team.'

As audiences move to digital platforms, YouTube is the big thing for advertising. Due to Prajakta's rising popularity, many brands reach out to her for collaboration. To consider the collaboration, she looks for alignment of three factors: i) What the brand wants from her; ii) Whether the brand content fits seamlessly into her content and content sensibilities; iii) What her audience is getting—are they getting what they came to her for? When these three factors align, she moves ahead.

Prajakta got her first brand collaboration opportunity after gaining 100,000 subscribers. For Yatra.com, she created a fortnightly property called *Mostly Yatra* on her channel. Through this series, she imparted her Yatra *gyaan*, or knowledge, with her witty take on being a traveller. She created videos on topics such as types of people on a road trip and types of Indian travellers.

Prajakta believes that online audiences are over the era of direct marketing, and simple ads do not engage them. She says, 'Today's audience is making conscious decisions. They choose where they want to spend their time. We need to respect their smartness.' Over the years, Prajakta has worked on many interesting brand collaborations, but she has never compromised on any communication that goes up on her channel as she knows that a bad inclusion will inevitably leave a dent.

IN CONCLUSION

Ambitious people who suffer career setbacks often experience episodes of shock, denial and self-doubt. It is hard for them to believe they may have failed in their chosen field. But failure can come to anyone, anytime and for numerous reasons. Prajakta's journey teaches us that even a career failure can be the beginning of new success if you respond correctly. The secret of making your comeback is to convert the frustration about past failures into enthusiasm about future possibilities.

Perspectives from Prajakta Koli

- Don't pretend to be someone else. Be yourself. You are a small part of the audience's life, so be honest. People like authenticity.
- If you are in the field of content creation, then you are in a long race. Take care of your health.
- You are changing, the world is changing, audiences are changing. Don't get monotonous. Don't get comfortable with something. Keep trying new things. Keep experimenting.
- Don't take your school and college life for granted. It is more than your marksheet. You will always remember your school and college days for the relationships you built, the jokes you shared and so much more.
- No two individuals can be the same. Therefore, you can cut competition by having your individual take on content.
- When you start, don't focus on numbers. Just focus on content. Content is king. If you figure that out, everything else will fall into place.

RANVEER ALLAHBADIA

RANVEER ALLAHBADIA

From Fitness Enthusiast to One of India's Most Popular Podcasters

When you really want something, the whole universe conspires in helping you to achieve it.

—Paulo Coelho

The inspiring story of the film *Lakshya* resonates with many a youngster who does not know what to do in life. In this film, Hrithik Roshan plays the role of an aimless young man, Karan Shergill, who has a laidback attitude towards everything in life. One day, a friend tells Karan he is joining the army. Imitating his friend, Karan too, applies to the Indian Military Academy (IMA) without discussing it with his parents and is selected. His friend backs out at the last moment. Alone, Karan finds it difficult to cope with the strict training regimen. One night, he runs away from the academy. Because of this act, Karan loses respect in the eyes of his father and girlfriend. The later part of the film shows the transformation of the careless Karan into a responsible soldier who fights and helps to win the crucial Kargil war by capturing an enemy-occupied peak (his *lakshya*, or aim). In the end, Karan not only earns the respect of his family, but also that of his country.

One of the essential lessons of the film is that you cannot achieve anything without a goal. But once you have a goal, you can climb the most challenging mountain in the world. Interestingly, there are many similarities between the story of Karan Shergill and Ranveer Allahbadia. During his teenage years, Ranveer was not sure what he wanted to do with his life. But today, he is one of the biggest youth influencers in India. As of April 2024, his YouTube channels *BeerBiceps* and *Ranveer Allahbadia*, available in English and Hindi respectively, have over 15 million subscribers. Another 6 million people follow him on other social media channels such as Instagram, X and LinkedIn. He also has several supplementary channels on YouTube, including *TRS Clips*, *TRS Clips Hindi*, *Best of TRS*, *Best of TRS Hindi*, *RAAAZ by BigBrainco*, *RAAAZ Clips* and *BeerBiceps Tamil*, collectively amassing more than 6 million followers.

Ranveer wears many hats. He hosts India's top-ranked podcast—*The Ranveer Show*, on which he has interviewed the likes of Priyanka Chopra, Saif Ali Khan, Rajkummar Rao, Boman Irani, Ayushmann Khurrana, Sri Sri Ravi Shankar and even his idol, Arnold Schwarzenegger. He has written for marquee newspapers, acted in a popular music video and endorsed numerous brands. In 2017, he and his college mate, Viraj Sheth, founded a digital entertainment company, Monk Entertainment (Monk-E). The company manages some of India's top digital talent. It has won numerous awards, including Bootstrapped Business of the Year at the Entrepreneur Awards 2020. Ranveer also co-founded Level Supermind, a meditation and wellness app, alongside Harshil Karia from Schbang in 2021. In 2022, he co-founded BeerBiceps Foundation, a silent arm under BeerBiceps that believes in giving back to society. In 2024, he established BeerBiceps Skillhouse to help people master the skills needed to become successful content creators and influencers. At the National Creators Award 2024, Ranveer received the Disruptor of the Year award from Prime Minister Narendra Modi.

So, are you wondering how a boy who was once clueless in life became one of the most popular youth influencers? Read on. Here is the story of Ranveer finding *his lakshya* and transforming himself.

THE BEGINNING

Ranveer was born on 1 June 1993, into a family of doctors. His grandparents, parents, and now his sister and brother-in-law, are doctors. As a child, he attended the Dhirubhai Ambani International School and was a top student. He was also very active in co-curricular activities like debate, drama and judo. At school, he became good friends with a girl and started dating her. Many love stories are not easy, and neither was Ranveer's.

In Class XII, he went through an ugly break-up with his girlfriend. A new relationship also did not work out. Feeling the pain of these broken relationships, he fell into a negative mindset. He began to drink and eat unhealthy restaurant food, and stopped studying. When he was sixteen, he was diagnosed with a stone in the gall bladder, which usually occurs in older people. In the next three years, he underwent two more surgeries. Prolonged bedrest after his surgeries and poor eating habits made him overweight. The boy who had once been a Bombay champion in judo became unfit for any sport.

But there is always a new dawn, even after the darkest night. Having hit rock bottom, Ranveer decided to adopt a healthy lifestyle to avoid future health issues. He eventually recovered.

Ranveer's parents were concerned about his career. Ranveer's father, Dr Gautam Allahbadia, is a globally renowned doctor, a successful medical entrepreneur and an acclaimed author.

His books and papers are considered compulsory reading for medical students. Because of Ranveer's aimless attitude and careless answers to his father's serious questions, stress grew between father and son. Dr Gautam Allahbadia wanted Ranveer to pursue medicine. But, following his friends, Ranveer decided on DJ Sanghvi College of Engineering.

Ranveer's troubles were far from over. His glamorous perception of engineering shattered when he found engineering subjects very dull. Eventually, he failed in one subject. Ranveer had always been top of his class, and it was difficult for him to accept this failure. He felt he had failed in his love life, his health and now education. Negative thoughts began to occupy his mind, and unknowingly, he went into depression. He was so disappointed with himself that one day, he thought of committing suicide. His mother, Dr Swati Allahbadia, sensed the situation and intervened, asking her son what he would like to do the next day. After some pushing from his mother, Ranveer expressed his desire to get a tattoo. Though Swati was not a fan of tattoos, she permitted Ranveer to do what he wanted. He got a phoenix tattoo on his left arm. Ranveer says, 'This tattoo symbolises a journey through fire or adversity. Whenever I look at this tattoo, it reminds me of the lowest period of my life.'

With his mother's moral support, Ranveer's mental state improved, and slowly he regained his lost self-confidence. He became serious about his studies again and began organising events and workshops in college. In line with his aspiration to do an MBA in finance, Ranveer did an internship with Ernst & Young. He survived the systems and processes, top-down decision-making and intense competition. But he found he was not comfortable taking orders from others. A corporate career was not for him.

After completing his engineering degree, Ranveer neither took up a job, nor did he pursue an MBA. His father noticed his lack of direction and asked him what he wanted to do. Ranveer replied, 'I want to be an entrepreneur.' He liked the art of cooking, so he was thinking of becoming a trained chef and opening a restaurant. Dubious, Dr Gautam Allahbadia described the challenges of running a restaurant business, but also the immense power of entrepreneurship. 'When I became an entrepreneur,' he told Ranveer, 'I had limited funds. Rather than asking my father for money, I chose to start from a garage. We had to struggle for a few years as we had limited patients. However, I wrote a few papers and books in that period. I got some international awards, which made me popular, and we started getting patients.'

Ranveer listened carefully to what his father was saying. 'For the next two years, I will allow you to do whatever you want to do with sincerity. The only thing is that you will not get any money from me, including pocket money.' Ranveer now had to figure out not only his passion, but also manage his expenses. Dr Swati Allahbadia, his mother, was worried about the situation. But Ranveer said to her, 'Mamma, one day Papa will be proud of me. Have faith in your son.'

There are many valuable lessons to be learnt from the evolution of Ranveer Allahbadia as a personal brand. Here are some of them.

SELF-AWARENESS IS THE FIRST STEP TOWARDS SUCCESS

Self-awareness is the ability to look at yourself and your life honestly. Ranveer thought he was most likely to succeed if he used his talents and passion to the fullest extent.

So, are you wondering how an overweight youngster who had undergone multiple surgeries, earned a six-pack?

In the second year of his engineering course, Ranveer decided to reduce his weight, which was 90 kg then. From some friends, he heard about Binny Sreedharan, a fitness coach. For the next three years, Ranveer trained under Binny and transformed his body. Although it may sound simple now, those three years were very tough for Ranveer. To keep himself motivated in his fitness journey, he would look at Arnold Schwarzenegger's poster at the gym and listen to his famous speech on the 'Six Rules of Success'.

Ranveer says, 'Whenever I want to bounce back in life, I listen to the motivational words of Arnold. He was born in a small village in Austria. When he chose bodybuilding, people shook their heads in disbelief. To everyone's surprise, he became Mr Universe at the age of twenty, and won the Mr Olympia title seven times. After becoming the most famous bodybuilder in the world, he decided to act in movies. But people criticised him for the way he looked and talked. But Arnold wasn't one to give up. He fought back hard, and within five years, he became one of the biggest Hollywood superstars of his time. Later, he wanted to work in the public service domain. Everyone said it would never happen; that he did not have the experience. But he was elected governor of California, not once but twice. From Arnold's journey, I have learnt to ignore naysayers, bounce back from setbacks, and put in efforts to become the absolute best in my field.'

Along with engineering, Ranveer had completed a certificate course from Peak Performance, a fitness academy run by his coach Binny Sreedharan. He looked at his hard-earned six-pack and thought of doing something related to fitness.

Having made up his mind to do something in the fitness field, Ranveer approached Binny Sreedharan to figure out possible opportunities. Following a deep discussion, the two of them planned to start a fitness venture, with an Uber-like model, for fitness and yoga coaches. They developed a basic app but needed to hire more people to scale up the pilot. When they took the idea to an investor, he suggested that for something like this to pick up, one of the co-founders needed to become popular. He suggested that they start a fitness channel on YouTube. Returning on Binny's scooter, Ranveer said, 'Let me achieve some perfection in video creation, and then I will start the channel. Maybe in the next few months.' To this, Binny replied, 'Just do it now, and improve on the go.'

There were many fitness videos already on YouTube, so Ranveer decided to do something different. In those days, YouTube did not have many videos by Indian fitness experts. In the few that existed, the video quality was poor. The problem with videos by foreign fitness experts was that they did not talk about the Indian vegetarian diet. Ranveer decided to create videos using high-quality cameras and target Indian audiences looking for a vegetarian fitness diet. His smartphone did not meet his quality bar and the high-end camera he wanted cost ₹38,000. He did not have the money, so he sold his favourite PlayStation and video games for ₹7,000. To arrange remaining ₹31,000, he went to Mumbai's famous Carter Road beach, where many wealthy people came to walk. He began pitching personal fitness training sessions to overweight people. Most ignored him, but then a few rich kids, impressed by his looks, muscles and speaking style, agreed to learn from him. Through these training sessions, Ranveer arranged the remaining amount and bought the required camera.

Ranveer began uploading videos on YouTube and, to promote his channel, he distributed pamphlets at places like Juhu Beach, Carter Road and Bandra Bandstand, in Mumbai. Through his videos, Ranveer started becoming famous, and many inquiries for fitness sessions began coming in. Soon, Ranveer was required to travel to various parts of Mumbai for training sessions. Earlier, he would travel in his father's BMW, but on this journey of self-discovery, he decided to buy a local train pass. Many of his friends and relatives laughed at him, but Ranveer ignored them. When he started earning more, he shifted from the second-class compartment to the first class.

While Ranveer was juggling multiple things, he and Binny realised there were many loopholes in their fitness venture's business model. By this time, Ranveer had begun to enjoy his YouTube journey, so they decided to close the fitness venture at the pilot stage.

To focus on his channel, Ranveer had also quit as a personal trainer. This decision turned out to be the right one. After a year of running his YouTube channel, he was making decent money through his training sessions. One day, he received ₹25,000 from Google AdSense (a platform that runs ads on YouTube). He realised there was long-term potential in scaling up his YouTube channel. Ranveer has become very popular through his channel and it made sense for him to focus on that.

Due to his popularity, passion for fitness and devotion to Arnold Schwarzenegger, in 2019, Disney sent him to South Korea to interview Arnold. Ranveer could hardly believe it. He says, 'Meeting Arnold Schwarzenegger was a dream come true. This is the power of the universe.'

ATTRACT PEOPLE TO JOIN YOUR MISSION

Remember that there is limited time available every day, and one person cannot handle all the work. While an entrepreneurial journey can start with a single person, it cannot scale up without the support of others. Ranveer was fitness-training multiple clients as a solo entrepreneur and devoting 3 hours a day to video creation. The person who shot Ranveer's videos was quite irregular. One day, Ranveer had planned an urgent video shoot, but the videographer did not turn up. Ranveer waited for almost an hour, and then, out of sheer frustration, called his childhood friend Zervaan for help.

Zervaan immediately came and shot the video. He understood Ranveer's frustration and introduced him to Rajas Pardeshi, a professional photographer. As Ranveer had limited funds, he told Rajas, 'For now, I can pay you only ₹200 per shoot. As my channel grows, I will make sure your payment also grows.' Rajas agreed. Within a few months, Ranveer had increased Rajas' payment to ₹7,000 per month, and later to ₹25,000 per month.

With Rajas' support, Ranveer grew *BeerBiceps* to 100,000 subscribers. Now, he felt he had a significant audience base and could approach brands for influencer marketing. He was looking for someone to help him get the brand deals, when he got a call from Viraj Sheth, a fellow alumnus from his engineering college, but two years his junior. As a final year student and member of the college's entrepreneurship cell, Viraj was organising an event and wanted Ranveer to speak there.

There is an interesting backstory. When Viraj joined the college, he was a shy person, and Ranveer was a very popular senior who hosted many of the events at the college. Viraj felt that if he had to improve his public speaking and communication skills, he had to associate with Ranveer. During the freshers' party, Ranveer hosted an event. During dinner, Viraj approached him but his hands were shaking from nervousness and the food on his plate fell onto Ranveer's friend. Seeing this, Ranveer got angry. Filled with fear, Viraj apologised and hurriedly left the place. Later, Viraj sent a friend request to Ranveer on Facebook, and Ranveer accepted.

When Ranveer got an internship opportunity in which he had to sell a course on financial markets, he looked around for a few juniors to help him, and recalled Viraj. Considering it to be a starting point to learn from Ranveer, Viraj joined him. Viraj remembers, 'At the time, the movie *The Wolf of Wall Street* was very popular among students, and we referenced it in our pitch.' Together, they sold ₹5 lakh worth of courses in the college itself. This was the highest revenue number ever achieved by the course company in any single college. After this internship, Ranveer and Viraj became good friends and even after Ranveer graduated, they remained in touch.

Coming back to Viraj's speaking invitation to Ranveer, after his talk at the college event, Ranveer asked Viraj about his plans. Viraj said he wanted to go to the US to do his MS, if he could get a scholarship. He also said he was interested in doing an MBA, but was not confident about getting into a top MBA college. Ranveer told Viraj about the upcoming wave of influencer marketing. Viraj was impressed by Ranveer's pitch but said that he belonged to a middle-class family, and doing a job or going for higher studies on a scholarship were the only two options for him. Ranveer offered him the opportunity to join as an intern and take a cut on the brand deals he brought in. Ranveer recalls, 'Viraj had never done anything related to brand deals, but I just knew he was a smart Gujarati guy who could bargain well, so I got him on board. He has achieved much beyond what I had expected at that time.'

Viraj says, 'Ranveer is a go-getter. His vision of creating an influencer marketing business was inspiring. He comes from an affluent family, but instead of enjoying the comforts through his parents' money, he was working hard to create a name for himself. I liked his hunger and said yes to the opportunity.' Viraj's GRE score being low, he had to give up on his dream of a

US scholarship, but while working with Ranveer as an intern, he got a job through college placements. He took the job, and supported Ranveer in whatever extra time he had during the day. By the time Viraj had completed three months on the job, he had made more money in brand deals than his salary from the job. So, in November 2017, Viraj convinced his parents that this was the right move and quit his job to join Ranveer full time.

After Viraj joined the team, the business started growing significantly, and new team members started joining the business. The office space grew from a room in Ranveer's parental home, to a garage, to a commercial office space in South Mumbai.

INCREASE YOUR CHANCES OF MEETING ACHIEVERS

LinkedIn founder Reid Hoffman said, 'The fastest way to change yourself is to hang out with people who are already the way you want to be.' The philosophy behind these words has played an instrumental role in Ranveer's journey. When he was starting his YouTube journey, Tanmay Bhat, co-founder of All India Bakchod (AIB), was one of the most popular digital celebrities in India. Tanmay had made it to the list of *Forbes*' Richest Celebrities 2016, rubbing shoulders with silver-screen stars like Shah Rukh Khan and Amitabh Bachchan.

In those days, Tanmay was overweight. Ranveer dropped him a message on Facebook with a link to his YouTube channel, which had 2,000 subscribers then. When he received no response, Ranveer messaged a few more times. Eventually, Tanmay responded. Ranveer helped Tanmay to lose about 110 kg. In return, Tanmay became Ranveer's first mentor in the digital media industry. He guided Ranveer on the business essentials and mindset needed to achieve success. He also educated Ranveer about influencer marketing, which had become prominent in the US and was about to start in India. He suggested Ranveer become an early mover in the space.

For his YouTube channel, Ranveer interviewed Vishal Gondal, founder of the fitness start-up GOQii. Vishal was also considered the poster boy of the Indian video gaming industry. His first company, Indiagames, was acquired by The Walt Disney Company. Vishal helped Ranveer define a big vision for the business. Ranveer says, 'Meeting Vishal gave me a lot of hope. I started feeling that I could achieve something big. Although I couldn't follow all the things he suggested, some of his advice has been very effective.'

Have you heard about Soho House? Founded in London, it is a private members' only club for those in film, media and creative industries. In Mumbai, Soho House is located on Juhu Beach. In order to meet the achievers in the creative sector, Ranveer became a member of Soho House. One day, he happened to meet Siddharth Roy Kapur, producer of some of the most successful Bollywood films such as *Dangal*, *Chennai Express* and *Taare Zameen Par*. Ranveer approached Siddharth to interview him for his YouTube channel. Siddharth agreed, and their relationship grew with time. Ranveer says, 'Siddharth has been kind to mentor me on several occasions. He has shared with me valuable lessons on growing a media business and has helped me come out of some personal issues.'

Ranveer has given a few TEDx talks. While in the greenroom for a TEDx event, he happened to meet Kiran Khalap, MD and co-founder of chlorophyll, a top-notch brand consulting firm. Kiran liked Ranveer's enthusiasm and passion for creating a powerful brand. The deep discussion with Kiran during the event turned into a long-term mentoring relationship. Ranveer says, 'Discussions with Kiran have helped me in multiple ways, including refining my approach to brand creation.'

In the dynamic and overly competitive business world, it is normal for an entrepreneur to have self-doubt. Having achieved decent growth for a few years, Ranveer's YouTube channel numbers began to stagnate. He could not understand why and began to lose his self-confidence. During this phase, Dr Radhakrishnan Pillai, a management guru and bestselling author of books on Chanakya's teachings, helped Ranveer understand his self-worth. With Dr Pillai's guidance, Ranveer was able to regain the growth he was looking for. Ranveer says, 'Different mentors have helped me during different stages of my journey. I keep meeting new achievers, and a few of them agree to mentor me.'

GROW YOUR INNER SELF THROUGH SPIRITUAL PRACTICES

In childhood, Ranveer used to make fun of people who talked about spirituality and meditation. But then a turning point came in his own life. In the final year of engineering, Ranveer listened to a podcast by Graham Hancock, a British writer who specialised in unconventional theories involving ancient civilisations. Through the podcast, Ranveer heard about Ayahuasca, a herbal drink made from plants that grow in the Amazon forests of South America. Over time, Ayahuasca has become popular among those who seek a way to heal past traumas. After listening to the podcast, Ranveer's perspective on spirituality changed.

Since he had graduated in engineering but was about to start *BeerBiceps*, people around Ranveer were doubtful about the wisdom of his decision. A career as a YouTuber was unheard of then. Seeing this, Ranveer became filled with self-doubt. One night, Ranveer's father came to his room and said, 'Once you start your entrepreneurial journey, you will get very busy. Let's go for a family vacation.' Dr Gautam Allahbadia had planned a vacation in the Seychelles, an island republic popular for its beautiful beaches. Ranveer agreed to join in.

During the trip, his father asked him to explore the beaches and spend time alone. One day, Ranveer was sitting on the beach alone when he happened to meet a European man. They started talking about various things, including spirituality. The subject of Ayahuasca appeared in the conversation, and Ranveer heard that the European was a Ayahuasca healer (a *shaman*). When Ranveer remarked that to experience Ayahuasca, one had to go to South America, the *shaman* replied that Ayahuasca could be experienced in Seychelles too. Ranveer had heard about fake *shamans* and got a little worried. He changed the subject and then left the place.

Over the next two days, Ranveer met that *shaman* on different occasions. He wondered how and why the meetings and conversations were happening. When Ranveer went for a deep-sea dive in the ocean, he recalled that in the podcast he had listened to, Graham Hancock had said that you don't go to Ayahuasca, it comes to you. By the time he emerged from the ocean, he had made up his mind to go on an Ayahuasca journey with the *shaman*. Ranveer says, 'It was a wonderful spiritual experience. I have covered it in detail in my podcast.'

After returning to India, Ranveer got busy with his regular workout at the gym, training his clients and building up his YouTube channel. Somehow, he had forgotten about continuing his spiritual learning. One day, out of the blue, Ranveer met the same *shaman* he had met in the Seychelles in Mumbai. During their conversation, the *shaman* suggested Ranveer do *AUM (OM)* chanting for 20 minutes every day. He said it would give him inner strength and quicken his recovery from surgical wounds. Following the advice, Ranveer started doing daily *AUM* chanting. Later, he also did Reiki, a Japanese technique of stress reduction and relaxation.

In 2017, Ranveer visited the office of TEDx in Mumbai as a potential speaker. He shared his speech with Manish Pandey, then a key member of the speaker selection team. Manish was very critical about Ranveer's speech and asked tough questions on every line. For instance, Ranveer had written, 'I have all the comfort at home, but I am struggling.' To this, Manish asked, 'What's special about that? People live below flyovers and struggle in life.' Ranveer thought Manish was an arrogant person. He suggested that Manish practise meditation and Reiki. Suddenly, Manish began to laugh and shared his background with Ranveer.

Manish had been actively practising meditation since his maternal grandfather introduced him to it at the age of five. He and Ranveer spoke for an hour on spirituality and various meditation practices. Realising Manish's deep knowledge, and being already familiar with the story of Manish's journey from a small village in Nepal to becoming a digital media expert, not only surprised Ranveer but increased his respect. Though Ranveer was not shortlisted as a speaker in that TEDx event, he and Manish became good friends. When Ranveer was leaving the TEDx office, Manish gifted him a book: *Autobiography of a Yogi*.

The book takes the reader on a journey into the spiritual adventures of Paramahansa Yogananda, an Indian monk, who introduced millions to meditation and the teachings of *Kriya Yoga*. One of the most famous readers of the book was Steve Jobs, the co-founder of Apple. He first read it as a teenager, and used to re-read the book once a year ever since. Ranveer says, 'Due to my hectic schedule, it took me a year to complete the book. It inspired me deeply, and I became fascinated with Indian culture and philosophy.' Ranveer stopped eating non-vegetarian food, which was once a part of his daily diet.

To go deeper into spirituality, Ranveer searched for Self-Realization Fellowship (SRF), the organisation founded by Paramahansa Yogananda. Surprisingly, he found an SRF centre close to his home. In 2018, Ranveer joined SRF, and has been doing 2 hours of meditation every day.

Ranveer says, 'The world of an influencer is filled with glamour. But the desire to meet the audience's expectations creates a lot of anxiety. And it hurts when people don't like your work and share hatred on social media. Practising meditation maintains my emotional balance through the highs and lows.' Interestingly, Ranveer has interviewed India's topmost spiritual gurus, Sri Sri Ravishankar, Jaggi Vasudev (Sadhguru), and Gaur Gopal Das on his YouTube channel.

ELEVATE YOUR TEAM

Ranveer says, 'One of my biggest role models is American basketball superstar LeBron James. Along with growing himself, he has elevated his basketball team, and has created many businesses that are run by his friends. Like him, I also want to elevate other people around me.'

Initially, Ranveer was creating only fitness-related videos, but when Rajas came on board, he started thinking of other ways and means to grow his channel so that he could pay Rajas better. The duo started experimenting with new video ideas. Earlier, Ranveer would post two fitness-related videos a week, one on Thursday, and the other on Saturday. They decided to post videos on some new topics on Thursdays. The first nine videos on communication skills, dating tips, etc., did not get much traction. But the tenth video on fashion emerged as a game changer. In a single day, the video gained almost ten times the views the fitness videos were getting in a week.

Looking at the numbers, Ranveer realised the potential of fashion videos. Also, there were limited brand deals available in the fitness space. But opportunities in the fashion space were immense. Over time, *BeerBiceps* evolved from a fitness channel to a lifestyle channel, and today, the name Ranveer Allahbadia is synonymous with fitness, fashion, motivation, health and lifestyle content on YouTube. Along with Ranveer, Rajas too, has grown tremendously. Today, he is the creative head and gets a share of *BeerBiceps*' brand deals revenue, which goes into lakhs of rupees.

Ranveer gives Viraj a lot of credit for creating the flow of brand deals. While working with *BeerBiceps* as an intern, the first brand deal Viraj cracked was with an energy drink brand, which paid ₹7,500 for a couple of Instagram posts. Although it was a small amount, for Viraj it was a big confidence booster. In the next few months, he collected the email IDs of the CEOs of 300 famous brands and sent them emails proposing brand deals with *BeerBiceps.* Viraj recalls that only three CEOs responded. One of them was the CEO of Tinder, the famous dating app. Through association with Tinder, the team earned more than ₹1 lakh.

To manage brand deals separately from *BeerBiceps*, in 2017, Ranveer and Viraj founded another agency, Monk Entertainment (Monk-E). Viraj knew that all brands worked with different PR and advertising agencies. He felt that if he could network with these agencies, he could get multiple clients from each one. Using the Tinder work reference, Viraj started approaching agencies.

He prepared a list of all the jargon used by agency people and prepared a pitch on how influencer marketing could add value in terms of increasing brand reach at a cost lower than other marketing channels. Initially, he was nervous, and many agencies ignored him as a kid. But, after a few trials, Viraj became comfortable in striking up a conversation. By this time, *BeerBiceps* had 350,000 subscribers, and agencies had begun to notice Viraj. Soon, brands like Puma, Jockey and Skechers came on board. The video for Skoda generated more than 1 million views, and the brand got many leads for the test drive. This success opened up doors with other brands. The Aditya Birla Group was looking for a young influencer who could talk about its financial products. Viraj liked the opportunity as the brand was also going to put up billboards at major airports and malls. Ranveer appeared as a model on those billboards.

Having gained some experience in the field, Viraj realised that the influencer marketing sector was completely disorganised. There was hardly anyone doing the background work for influencers. He had also made many influencer friends who required the services he was running for Ranveer. So Viraj and Ranveer decided to extend Monk-E services to other influencers also. In this way, Monk-E began working with many influencers and brands. Ranveer and Viraj soon realised that even brands did not completely understand how the world of influencer marketing worked. Given that the Monk-E team had solid knowledge in the field, the company began handling the influencer marketing projects of various brands. Viraj says, 'Today, we handle influencers as well as run influencer campaigns. We also help brands with their entire social media and digital strategy.'

Over time, Viraj also developed connections with agencies involved with Bollywood stars. Viraj and Ranveer discussed the opportunities for interviewing Bollywood personalities at the newly created interview property *The Ranveer Show*. Ranveer suggested they start with a popular name as that would help in positioning the show. Initially, Viraj could not get a big Bollywood name, but somehow, he arranged an interview opportunity with cricketer Virat Kohli. Unfortunately, the opportunity fell through and the meeting with Virat did not happen. Then Viraj arranged an interview opportunity with Hrithik Roshan. This too fell through. Finally, Viraj received a call from a contact regarding an opportunity to interview Priyanka Chopra. Though Viraj prepared the interview questions, because of the previous experiences, he was not too hopeful it would in fact, happen.

As luck would have it, Viraj and Ranveer got a slot to interview Priyanka at Mehboob Studio, where she was shooting for the film, *The Sky Is Pink*. The meeting was delayed for 2 hours, and the duo began to think history was repeating itself. But suddenly, Priyanka appeared, and Ranveer proceeded to interview her. The popularity of this video created a lot of pull for *The Ranveer Show*, and opportunities to interview many other stars emerged.

Viraj says, 'The experience of establishing Monk-E has made me realise that even if you are new to the industry and people don't take you seriously, you should not be scared of anyone. Self-confidence and the hunger to learn can open the doors eventually.'

Within a short period, Monk-E has collaborated with brands such as Gillette, Pantene, Nykaa Man, OYO, Nokia, Celio and others. It has also handled several movie and music promotion campaigns for large companies such as Sony Music and Reliance Entertainment. Ranveer says, 'We are just starting. We are as hungry as we were on day one.' Monk-E is now investing in creating many more sub-brands that will be handled by passionate leaders like Viraj. Ranveer says, 'The way people say Apple came out of a garage in America and Alibaba came out of a small apartment in China, my dream is that one day, people will say that some of the biggest companies came out of a YouTube channel in India.'

IN CONCLUSION

In the movie *Lakshya*, on the night before his final attempt at capturing the peak by rock-climbing, Karan (Hrithik Roshan) calls his father (Boman Irani). Karan was not sure whether he would return from the battle, hence he wanted to smooth things over with his father and have a heart-to-heart conversation. When his father tells him that his mother is not at home, Karan replies that he has called to speak to him. His father hears him quietly weeping, and asks if Karan is alright. Karan says that his father has given him so much in life, but all he has given his father is grief. His father replies, 'There was a time I was upset with you, but today I'm proud of you, very proud.'

In similar vein, Ranveer too, has kept his promise to his mother. Today, Ranveer's father is a proud man.

Perspectives from Ranveer Allahbadia

- If you are passionate about a field but afraid to start your own venture, then learn the traits of that field by becoming an intern or executive assistant to a person who is a leading star in the field.
- Whatever you have in your heart, do it with 100 per cent sincerity. Our own self-doubt is the biggest roadblock to our success.
- If you want to become an entrepreneur in the content field, then create a content publishing timetable and follow it with discipline. Also, keep an eye on evolving trends and audience tastes. Consistency in your publishing schedule and continuous reinvention of your content can take you to the desired heights.
- In whatever field you want to make your mark, make knowledge your differentiating factor.
- If you are good at something, don't become overconfident and arrogant about your craft. Keep your hunger for perfection alive and surround yourself with humble people.
- Don't listen to people who doubt your potential. However, do listen to people who give you feedback on your development needs.

MADAN GOWRI

MADAN GOWRI

From MNC Employee to One of the Biggest Digital Influencers of South India

Adversity causes some men to break; others to break records.
—William Arthur Ward

Think back for a moment to a setback you have experienced in your life. Everyone on this planet has had one at one point or another. But how people react to setbacks differs a lot. Some let it push them into a negative spiral. Others make it a stepping stone to something better. This is the story of someone who belongs to the latter category.

A few years ago, like many other youngsters, Madan was dealing with relationship problems. In March 2016, he was talking on the phone to his girlfriend, who was hundreds of kilometres away. The conversation went in the wrong direction and a small problem escalated into a big one. Upset, Madan's girlfriend disconnected the call.

Madan tried calling her back, but found she had blocked his number. Seeing a message from her on WhatsApp, he opened it eagerly. It was an offensive middle finger emoji. Upset, Madan fell asleep on the sofa. The next morning, he tried messaging his girlfriend on WhatsApp, but she had blocked him. Then he tried messaging her on Facebook, but he was unfriended there too.

Desperately, he tried all social networks both were connected to, but he had been blocked everywhere.

Not having any other way to contact his girlfriend, Madan created an apology video and posted it on YouTube. Although the girl did not respond, others did! This was the first time Madan had been appreciated for something by the public. While going through break-up depression, Madan discovered YouTube as a platform for self-expression and a way to redirect his energy. Gradually, he began posting more videos. But his channel subscribers did not increase. He even went to a temple and prayed for double-digit subscribers on his YouTube channel. But for a long time, the number did not move beyond nine. Frustrated, he even created another account and subscribed to achieve ten subscribers.

Today, Madan Gowri is one of the biggest digital influencers of South India. As of April 2024, Madan had over 10 million followers on various social media platforms such as YouTube, X, Facebook and Instagram. He has received numerous awards, including Best Vlogger of the Year from Black Sheep. Apart from producing his own videos, Madan has interviewed many celebrities, including cricketer Harbhajan Singh and author Chetan Bhagat. He has also given a popular TEDx talk and co-created India's first animated emoji-based (AniMojis) viral song, 'Monkeys with 5G'.

But Madan's success did not come overnight. He has had his share of painful days and sleepless nights. This is Madan's story, how an unknown middle-class boy became a household name to every Tamilian out there.

THE BEGINNING

Madan was born in 1993, in Madurai, the cultural capital of Tamil Nadu. His father worked with an NGO, and his mother was a government employee. So he grew up in a hardworking middle-class family. After studying for a few years in Madurai, he gained admission to Sainik School, Amaravathinagar, one of twenty-five Sainik schools in India.

The Sainik School experience broadened Madan's perspective and exposed him to many co-curricular activities such as boxing, debating, drumming, hockey and football. Madan says, 'I tried multiple things in school, but never got an opportunity to get on the main stage, as I was always rejected in the preliminary rounds.' He was not drawn to engineering, but like most middle-class kids, he took the exam and was selected. After his engineering degree, Madan worked for some time with Cognizant, a leading IT company. He then did an MBA in India, and MS in the US.

Madan could have stayed on in the US, but chose to return to India. He loves the energy that comes from the chaos and confusion that is India. In contrast, the US was organised and somewhat boring for him. Madan says, 'People go to museums, they live at home. I travel to many countries. They all are like museums. And for me, my country is my home.'

Back in India, Madan started working with Zoho, one of India's largest software service (SaaS) companies. He loved his job, but as a side hustle, he focused on building his YouTube channel. He soon found that by setting aside a few hours a day he could not do justice to his channel. So he promised himself he would quit his job after achieving 1 million subscribers. On 8 September 2018, Madan's channel achieved that number. But it took him a few months to adjust to the idea of leaving his well-paying job. Finally, he convinced his parents he would like to pursue his passion full-time. Call it youthful exuberance or naivety, but Madan felt he was making the right choice. And with perseverance, Madan made things work. There was no looking back.

There are many valuable lessons to be learnt from the evolution of Madan Gowri as a personal brand. A few of them are shared here.

HAVE ROLE MODELS

Usually, when people want to do something in life, they look at their peers, neighbours, friends and family and define the boundaries of their dreams accordingly. Madan says, 'If you want to do something new, look at the people who changed the world.' He believes that reading about the work of great people, whom you have not even met, can inspire you to achieve incredible things. Madan wanted to do something different, something that had not been done before by his friends and family members. So he looks to three leaders for inspiration.

The first is Steve Jobs. Steve had no known family name, no parental wealth and no fancy college degree. Before co-founding Apple, he experimented a lot. He dropped out of college after six months and spent the next eighteen months in creative classes. In 1974, he took a position as a video game designer. After a few months, he left the company to seek spiritual enlightenment in India.

Reviewing this part of Steve Jobs' life, many people would have called him directionless. Later, the same person revolutionised the personal computer industry. After Apple's IPO, he became one of the youngest millionaires in the world. Reviewing this part of Steve's life, many people would have called him lucky. And then, strange but true, he was fired from his own company. But even after all the devastating setbacks, Steve made a spectacular comeback. He created Pixar, which redefined animation movies. Eleven years after Steve was fired, Apple was on the brink of bankruptcy. Steve came back and turned it into the world's most valuable company. Reviewing this part of his life, most people would call him a comeback champion.

The second is Swami Vivekananda. When India was still under British rule, and the Western world had not recognised the Indian genius in many fields, Swami Vivekananda brought Hinduism to the world status as a major world religion. In 1893, the World Parliament of Religions was organised in Chicago, USA. Without an invitation, Swami Vivekananda reached America to attend. His speeches shook America and the world. Swami Vivekananda became a star in America. It was a matter of pride for India that one of our own had gone to America and impressed the whole world with his simplicity, genius and exceptional authority. His achievements filled the people of India with self-confidence, positivity and hope.

The third is Dr B.R. Ambedkar. The architect of the Indian constitution was born in a poor Dalit family. Growing up, he faced segregation because of his caste. He was made to sit apart from his classmates in a corner. Nor was he allowed to touch the water tap from which the others drank. His family lived in one room. He would wake up at 2 a.m. to study, as the household was quiet then. With hard work and determination, he became the first Indian to go abroad to pursue a doctorate in economics. He studied at Columbia University and the London School of Economics. Later, he was India's first law and justice minister and played an essential role in protecting the rights of Dalits in the country. But he will be forever primarily known as the man who wrote the democratic constitution of India, by which millions of Indians live today.

None of the three role models he chose were related to Madan's field of work, but he felt very much connected to all of them. He says, 'The problems we are facing are nothing compared to what they faced. They had immense self-belief. They did things they wanted to do, and history remembers them for the change they brought.' Inspiration from these role models keeps driving Madan to pursue his passion and make an impact.

DARE TO BE DIFFERENT

Steve Jobs changed the way many electronic devices looked and worked. In life and in business, he followed Apple's advertising slogan: *Think Different*. The slogan has inspired many people to challenge the status quo. Madan is one of them.

When Madan arrived at the YouTube scene, there was plenty of English and Hindi content available on YouTube, but nothing much in Tamil. Initially, Madan too, shot his videos in English. But some viewers asked him to explain the same topic in Tamil. While accommodating their requests, Madan realised the massive potential of regional content. So he started creating Tamil videos. He also found that most Tamil videos on YouTube were about entertainment and politics, with little space devoted to information on social issues. So he decided to fill the void.

Madan focused on creating well-researched and extremely informative videos covering a wide range of topics ranging from current affairs to conspiracy theories, to science to politics to religion. He loves exploring stories from multiple dimensions and shares a different perspective on situations. Once he zeroes in on a topic, he researches extensively on the internet. If the subject demands it, he also contacts relevant people offline. The premise behind Madan's videos is simple. He condenses the appropriate information and presents the simplified version briefly.

At first, Madan created his perspectives on topics based on what had been written by others. But, over time, he realised that every author or publication had its own perspective and agenda, which should not influence his thoughts. He also realised that the presentation of history was not grounded in facts but the interpretation of events by authors who were usually influenced by the narrative of the victors. He even found that popular literature like the Ramayana has more than 300 versions, of which *Ram Charit Manas* by Tulsidas (Hindi), and *Kamba Ramayana* (Tamil), are the most popular. Based on the Ramayana version referred to, people hold different beliefs. For instance, many people worship Ram as a god/hero and consider Ravana a villain, but there are places in India where Ravana is considered a hero.

Madan says, 'Others' perspectives can influence your perspective, and when you get biased, you can offend people who think differently.' Hence, he decided to keep his content neutral and unbiased. Though Madan takes logical stances, he refrains from taking political sides.

One of the key differences between traditional media and online media is censorship. In internet videos, censorship does not apply. Therefore, on OTT platforms, there is a lot of content with nudity, violence and offensive language. Most of the content on online platforms cannot be enjoyed by the whole family, which is worrisome. Madan ensures that his content has no vulgarity, no abusive language, nor negative comments about anyone. He wants his content to be suitable for viewing by the whole family. He says, 'Audiences come to my platform for its positivity.' His value-based content focus has been a good decision. Due to his unconventional, interesting and informative content, Madan is now widely known in South India.

TAKE BABY STEPS TOWARDS CHANGING THE WORLD

Swami Vivekananda said, 'Take up one idea. Make that one idea your life; dream of it; think of it; live on that idea. Let the brain, the body, muscles, nerves, every part of your body be full of that idea and just leave every other idea alone. This is the way to success, and this is the way great spiritual giants are produced.'

In India, people listen to Bollywood stars, politicians and cricketers. Madan was none of these. But, on YouTube, people listened to him. So he felt he too could contribute to changing the world in some small way.

When someone is experimenting on an unknown path, he or she needs an encouraging friend or support group to be around. Madan had started creating videos while doing his MBA. He shared a hostel room with another student. A shy person, Madan was uncomfortable about shooting videos in his roommate's presence. As a supportive gesture, his friend would leave the room whenever Madan wished to shoot. The videos brought Madan little more than thirty or forty views from friends, but his roommate never discouraged him. He told Madan, 'When anything starts, it is insignificant. You should keep yourself positive and keep posting videos on YouTube.'

Due to his academic load of assignments and exams, it was difficult for Madan to focus on video creation. He shared his dilemma with his marketing professor, who listened to him patiently and advised Madan to sleep for just as long as his body required. Madan understood that one had to sacrifice extra sleep for one's passion. When we die, we can sleep for an indefinite period.

Even after putting in great effort, Madan's videos did not gain traction on YouTube. Then something happened that changed Madan's focus and his channel's traction. On 24 June

2016, Swathi, a twenty-four-year-old Infosys employee, was murdered at the Nungambakkam railway station in Chennai. Hearing about a young girl being murdered in broad daylight and unable to do anything about it made Madan restless. He chose to put out an emotional video on YouTube. Within 24 hours, the video received more than 50,000 views. Seeing the response, Madan began creating well-researched and extremely informative content on social issues. From menstruation to prostitution, he has covered many topics in his unique style.

Madan also seeks to grow social awareness about topics people shy away from discussing. For instance, in June 2020, P. Jeyaraj and his son J. Bennix died of alleged custodial torture in Sathankulam town, near Thoothukudi, in Tamil Nadu. A police investigation found severe injuries to their private parts. Madan expressed his thoughts through his YouTube channel and created awareness about the incident. In September 2020, Jothisri Durga, a nineteen-year-old medical aspirant, committed suicide. She was found hanging at her residence. She had left a suicide note saying she was apprehensive about the NEET exam though others had high hopes for her. Madan covered the incident and the issues around it.

As a country, India is welcoming of advanced technology. But when it comes to caste and religion, our society is still conservative and divided. To highlight this contrast, Madan collaborated with Tamil rapper Arivu. The duo developed the concept into a song and created a video titled 'Monkeys with 5G'. The song featured Arivu and Madan in animated form, taking jibes at people who think progressively but retain caste discrimination in their minds. It was the first Indian song to be shot entirely with the animated emojis (AniMojis) feature on the iPhone. The video went viral within a few days of its launch.

Madan says, 'We presented the song in a sarcastic and fun manner to trigger youngsters to talk about the issue and move casteism away from society.' Along the same lines, Madan has created a lot of content to inform and awaken people around various other social issues.

CONTINUOUSLY LEARN AND IMPROVE YOURSELF

Dr B.R. Ambedkar said, 'Cultivation of mind should be the ultimate aim of human existence.' Since childhood, Madan has been curious to know the why and how behind major events. He also loved simplifying complex topics by understanding them deeply. This curiosity and passion helped him in his entrepreneurial journey.

Madan says, 'Every day, there is new competition as millions of digital creators are entering the field. They are energetic, creative and hungry. The only way to stay relevant is to keep learning new things and unlearning the old things.'

Great content is created as a result of passion plus expertise. To develop his expertise in any topic he covers, Madan does a lot of homework. He reads and absorbs every single source he can find on the topic. Once the research is done, the content has to be presented in the form of an engaging story. For every video, he puts in a lot of preparation. Then he single-handedly produces his content, including shooting, editing, etc. When he started, he was not proficient in all the tools and technologies, but he spends a lot of time learning these things. He also reviews his audience's comments, to understand what they are looking for. Often, he gets great topic ideas from his audience.

The creative field does not merely demand preparation on the subject and the technical tools, it also requires deep learning on the emotional front. Sometimes, YouTubers see they have got just fifty views on a video and think they are no good and stop trying. On the other hand, when videos are watched by thousands, they believe they have made it and get into a comfort zone. Earlier on, Madan would think a great deal about the number of views, but later, he realised that as an artist one could not allow one's commitment to go up and down based on the audience size. Creator commitment has to remain strong and consistent.

Dislikes and negative comments are a significant part of the world of online videos. Earlier, Madan would get upset with dislikes and negative comments on his videos. Then he realised that in creative fields, ideas are appreciated by many, but also rejected by many. He has learnt that one should never enter a situation expecting a perfect result. He continuously learns from his audience feedback as well as YouTube analytics, trying to improve himself. He says, 'Dislikes should not destroy you; they should motivate you to improve. The good part about dislikes is that they keep you on your toes. They make sure that you don't float in a cloud.'

Memes are extensively used by teenagers to communicate in the digital world. People use memes to express emotions on platforms like Instagram, TikTok and Snapchat. Many times, people created funny and sarcastic memes of Madan. At first, he was offended. But over time, he learnt that memes are good for marketing. They help a person become more popular.

Madan explains, 'As an entrepreneur, you sometimes have a fantastic day, and sometimes you face adverse situations. You have to be calm even in the highest highs and the lowest lows. Don't get excited when things are going great, and don't get disheartened when things are going crap. If today is bad, tomorrow can be great and vice versa. Always keep an eye on your long-term goal.'

DON'T COMPROMISE ON YOUR VALUES

Advertisers go where the audience goes. In earlier times, the audience was on traditional channels such as television, movie screens, radio, magazines and newspapers, so advertisers were there. Now, the audience is moving towards digital media, so advertisers are also moving towards digital properties.

Most movie actors and online influencers do advertisements to supplement their income. Some believe it is quick and easy money. But unlike stars in North India, Tamil stars are conservative about brand endorsements. For instance, Amitabh Bachchan, Akshay Kumar and the Khans of Bollywood have endorsed numerous brands. But Rajinikanth has never lent his name to any brand endorsement. Kamal Haasan endorsed a brand for the first time recently, to support a good cause. He donated the fee he received from the endorsement towards the welfare of HIV-positive kids. Tamil superstars believe the value of their integrity is far greater.

Being a popular personal brand in the online world, especially in Tamil Nadu, Madan gets many offers for brand endorsements. Madan says, 'Values help you establish your sense of purpose and direction for your personal brand.' Like Tamil superstars, Madan too has chosen to be careful and conservative about brand endorsements. His philosophy is to give others what you will consume yourself, be it content or a branded product. If he is ethically against a particular concept, he does not endorse that brand.

For instance, an online gaming company approached Madan with a lucrative offer, but he was not comfortable with the concept of gambling and thought parents would not be pleased with their children putting money into gambling, so he let go the opportunity. He is active in the stock market and selectively talks about demat and stock trading brands such as Groww. He consumes content on Hotstar and has done ads for the brand. Even when he has not personally used the brand, he supports it only if he feels it is doing the right thing. For instance, Madan is a big believer in online education. Though he has not used upGrad, he has advertised it.

Madan says, 'One may feel compelled to take some of the first offers that come from brands. But one should wait. The more you focus on monetisation, the more you may lose focus on your audience.' Audiences come to Madan's channel because they trust him to be unbiased in his views. He says, 'There is a relationship between me and my audience, and I value the affection they have given me. In the short term, they might consider my advice on some brand, but if they don't find it authentic, they will ignore my thoughts in the long term.' He believes that if one has influence, one should not use it to influence people in the wrong way.

IN CONCLUSION

After facing rejection, people tend to become gloomy in their outlook and risk-averse. But rejections, setbacks and breakups are not the end of the road. They could be signals to change the road being travelled. Madan picked up the signal and created a new path for himself. His journey highlights that you must believe in yourself and your dreams. Who knows what surprising, successful and wonderful things you will end up doing?

Perspectives from Madan Gowri

- Respect your audience's time. Make every minute worthy of your audience. If someone is spending 5 minutes on your video, they should get value for every minute. Make your content that worthy.
- Be deaf to the opinions of others. Follow your vision. There will always be people who will throw their opinions at you. No one else can see your vision, no matter how great he or she is.
- Have intelligent friends as sounding boards. But don't have extra-intelligent friends who have problems with every solution you find in life. They will not allow you to make progress.
- Be consistent in what you do and stay persistent in what you want to achieve.
- If you are passionate about something, then jump off the cliff. But before you hit the ground, build a parachute (a financial cushion for you and your family). The feeling that you are going to hit the ground will push you to create a parachute faster.

SONAL DEVRAJ AND NICOLE CONCESSAO

SONAL DEVRAJ AND NICOLE CONCESSAO (Team Naach)

From Dance Teachers to Prominent Dancing Sensations

I didn't get there by wishing for it or hoping for it, but by working for it.

—Estée Lauder

All too often, people think the key to happiness is to earn more money and get fancy job titles. It turns out they are wrong. In reality, earning a livelihood from your passion is the best thing you can do for a healthy and enjoyable work life. Many people want to pursue their passions, but most of them do not know what to do.

This is the story of two talented girls, Nicole Concessao and Sonal Devraj, who turned their passion into a profession and created one of the country's most popular dance brands—Team Naach. Their enjoyable, diversified and straightforward choreographies appeal to a large global audience. They teach different dance styles such as Bollywood, Belly Fusion, hip-hop, semi-classical fusion and freestyle.Thousands of dance enthusiasts, especially women, have learnt from them via workshops, event choreographies, online tutorials and dance fitness routines.

By April 2024, more than 6 million people followed Team Naach across digital platforms, and their online videos had received over 7 billion views. Team Naach has performed continuously in YouTube FanFest, a gathering of some of the biggest YouTube stars from around the world. They have also collaborated with many international and Indian celebrities, including Alia Bhatt, Madhuri Dixit, Varun Dhawan, Sonam Kapoor and Will Smith. The list of Team Naach's achievements goes on. They have also collaborated with music labels, fashion designers and brands such as Disney, Honda, Google, Shoppers Stop and KFC.

But this passion-to-paycheck story has not been all smooth sailing. Sonal and Nicole have faced many roadblocks in their journey. There was a point when they had zero students in class and running the business was taking its toll on their finances and morale. There were other challenges too, including hiring good staff. But the roadblocks did not stop them. They figured out how to climb over, go through or work around them.

THE BEGINNING

Nicole and Sonal share similar stories. Nicole was born in Mumbai on 23 October 1989, but due to her father's job, the family moved to Lagos, Nigeria, when she was two years old. Though she grew up in Africa, her upbringing was very much influenced by Indian culture. She studied in a CBSE school and visited her grandmother in Mumbai every summer. Sonal was born in Chennai, on 4 September 1990, but moved with her family to Bahrain on account of her parents' work. She too, visited India frequently to be with her grandparents.

During their childhoods, both Sonal and Nicole received a thorough grounding in classical dance, as many Indian girls do. While Sonal trained in Bharatanatyam, which is a classical dance form that originated in South India, Nicole trained in Kathak, the classical dance form of the northern courts of Oudh and Agra. Coincidentally, both moved to India for their undergraduate studies, joining MMK College, Bandra, in Mumbai. They moved in different circles but became friends when they competed together as a team for college dance events. Following graduation, they opted for different careers. Sonal worked as a model and photographer, and Nicole tried her hand at marketing and PR.

One evening, the two girls were taking a walk in Khar, Mumbai, when they noticed a newly opened dance studio and decided to go in. They discovered the founder knew them through their college performances. He asked if they would like to teach a class at his studio. Since they both loved dance, they decided to teach a class on impulse. They enjoyed the session so much that they decided to continue to teach dance. In April 2014, they joined hands to start their own dance class—Team Naach—as a side hustle. In November 2016, they started their YouTube channel, to deliver content to their online audience.

There are many valuable lessons in the evolution of Team Naach as a brand. Here are a few.

FIGURE OUT YOUR PASSION

While the advice to pursue your passion is freely and frequently given, most people do not know what they are passionate about. Childhood provides a great opportunity to try a bit of everything, which helps in finding our talents and figuring out our true passions. Unfortunately, most children miss the opportunity to discover their non-academic talents due to the burden of academics. Not everyone can be a star academically.

However, children can be good at many other things that are not part of the syllabi but which can take them forward to a fulfilling life.

In the most popular TED talk of all time, Sir Ken Robinson made a case for creating an education system that nurtures rather than undermines creativity. Extracurricular activities help in the creative development of a child. Fortunately for them, both Sonal and Nicole's parents considered such activities as important as academics. Nicole says, 'Participation in various extracurricular activities along with my studies helped me learn to manage time, build people skills and improve my self-confidence. I also learnt to express myself in a better way.' Though Nicole took part in several extracurricular activities, she enjoyed dance the most.

There are numerous styles of dance and people dance for many reasons, to celebrate, compete, exercise and so on. Nicole says, 'Learning classical dance gives you a sense of discipline, rhythm and expression. So your base as a dancer gets strong.' Classical dance forms, such as Bharatanatyam and Kathak, are essential parts of Indian culture. Many Indian film stars who have won millions of hearts with their spectacular dance moves, are trained classical dancers. For instance, Sridevi was trained in Bharatanatyam and Kathak from childhood. Prabhudeva, the South Indian superstar, learnt several Indian classical dance forms, including Bharatanatyam. Madhuri Dixit started her training in Kathak when she was only three years old. Similarly, though Nicole grew up in Africa, her parents made sure she learnt Kathak. She also explored other dance forms and participated in every stage show and dance competition in school.

In Sonal's case, her grandmother helped her to explore her passion for dance. When she was in Class VI, she moved from Bahrain to India for a couple of years to stay with her grandparents. Sonal says, 'In South India, children are encouraged to pursue some form of art. So it was natural for my grandmother to encourage me to learn Bharatanatyam from an early age.' Later, Sonal decided she would like to master the art of dance. When she moved back to Bahrain, she began exploring different dance styles. With continuous practice, her body movements became elegant and effortless. Gradually, Sonal became an accomplished dancer.

OUR BELIEFS DRIVE OUR ACTIONS

Our beliefs about what we can and cannot do often limit our achievements. If you want to change your circumstances, skills and even your life, you often have to change your beliefs. The story of Hasil Adkins is one about the power of belief. Hasil Adkins was a one-man band. He could sing and simultaneously play various musical instruments such as the guitar, drums, piano, harmonica, etc. You must be thinking that people struggle to play even a single instrument, so how did Hasil Adkins play so many? The answer is belief.

As a child, he heard a song on the radio and the radio jockey say 'Hank Williams and others'. Just a child, Hasil assumed that one musician named Hank Williams played every instrument in the song. This assumption turned into a belief. He began to believe that he needed to play all the instruments if he wanted to become a music star. He taught himself to repair washing machines and cars so he could earn the money to feed his passion for music. Eventually, he became a cult figure among record collectors and musicians.

Sonal and Nicole too believed that once you had a foundation in classical dance, you could perform any dance form. Classical dance is a great way to train a dancer's awareness of storytelling, music and rhythm while dancing. By the time the two girls had reached college, they had learnt various dance styles such as hip-hop, jive, belly dance and Bollywood dance, and the three years in college gave them numerous opportunities to participate in dance competitions. Sonal says, 'At college, we met Dhawal Doshi, a famous choreographer-dancer. He was a great teacher then, and a big supporter of Team Naach now.'

Dancers do not just aimlessly hit poses and dance moves through the music. They are actually hitting accents and beats with a great sense of timing. Choreographers are the people who help dancers 'design' their dance by organising different moves into sequences and patterns according to a specific beat or melody. As Sonal and Nicole were trained in various dance styles, they were able to choreograph songs in different styles and make the fusion exceptional.

When choreographing a song, they listen to it many times and incorporate a range of styles from classical to modern. Since its inception, Team Naach has focused a lot on Bollywood dance routines. Because of the popularity of Bollywood songs and the viability of the Team Naach dance steps, people across India now identify with their choreography. Their semi-classical versions of popular songs have garnered a lot of traction. For instance, their belly fusion choreography of the song 'O Saki Saki', from the movie *Batla House*, was one of the most-watched videos on YouTube in 2019. By February 2021, this video had received over 58 million views. Their choreography on 'Makhna', from the movie *Drive*, became a rage, especially at *sangeets*, the wedding event in which family members and guests perform dance routines. In 'Ghar More Pardesiya', from the movie *Kalank*, Alia Bhatt and Varun Dhawan performed to Nicole and Sonal's classical dance moves. Without a doubt, the girls are now prominent dancing sensations on the internet.

STRUGGLES MAKE US STRONGER

When it comes to facing struggles, many people become disappointed and give up. But when they do persist, they begin to realise that struggles are part of the journey, preparation for take-off. After college, Sonal was runner-up in the Miss Kerala competition. It led to offers for a few Malayalam films. But, in her very first film, after the first schedule, the producers stopped responding to her. She realised they had decided to make the movie without her. She was heartbroken. Refusing to give up, she signed another film. Although the film did well, Sonal felt uncomfortable in the industry. Then, before she started shooting for her third film, the producer said suggestively, 'Madam, you have to adjust.' Offended, Sonal quit.

Turning away from films, Sonal applied for two jobs, but was not selected. She did not wish to be dependent on anyone, so she decided to try wedding photography. To mark her new journey, her father gifted her a camera. Sonal started as an assistant to a few famous wedding photographers. When one of them, Anant Singhal, realised that Sonal could also dance well, he referred her for a wedding choreography assignment. The client liked Sonal's work, and so word of mouth began to bring in more assignments. Slowly, college friends also began recommending her within their networks, and new clients kept on coming.

A few years later, Sonal met Nicole in Khar and they decided to go for a walk together. On impulse, they walked into a newly set up dance studio. Liking the place, they began teaching dance classes there on weekends. Gradually, they increased the class frequency from weekly to daily. Nicole was then in a Marketing and PR job, so she would teach after work. She says, 'I was putting in extra effort after office hours to teach others. However, dance is a mode of relaxation for me, so I didn't realise the effort.'

Quitting a full-time job takes courage and motivation. For more than a year, Nicole worked her day job and then taught dance in the evenings. Then she decided to quit her day job and focus entirely on her passion. She says today, 'While working at a job, I could not give 100 per cent to my passion. Nor was I able to give 100 per cent to my job. I felt it was time for me to move on from my 9 to 5 job.'

Quitting the job hit Nicole's finances. There were few students in the class, and the income inconsistent. Nicole says, 'Initially, seven or eight students came to our class. Gradually, the number dropped. There were times when we had no students.' The key reason for this drop was that people got bored easily or just wanted to learn the steps to one song. So the same group could not be retained. Also, due to the fierce competition, it was difficult to keep attracting new students. Sonal says, 'We had not followed the typical path of winning a dance reality show, and we were not famous as many of the other dance teachers were. So getting students beyond our friends circle was a challenge.'

In her childhood, Nicole's mother had taught her to be self-dependent. So asking for money from her parents was not an option. To cut her expenses, Nicole stopped socialising and shopping to a large extent. She says, 'My attitude of being financially independent was also influenced by my grandmother, who started her career as a teacher when studying was not the norm for girls. In time, she became the principal of the school. She became independent early in life, looked after herself and took care of her siblings. I have learnt many things from my grandmother. She is a strong woman.'

But there is always a flip side, and the good part about leaving her job was that Nicole now had more bandwidth. She began to think of ways to market the classes. To attract students,

Nicole posted a song on Facebook. She and Sonal had rendered Prabhudeva's 'Muqabala' in hip-hop, Kathak, and belly dance, and it received immense love online from friends and juniors in college. That Facebook video marked the initiation of Team Naach into the world of online dance.

However, starting their YouTube channel took some time. Nicole came across YouTube videos of international dancers and choreographers such as Matt Steffanina and Dana Alexa. Watching them, they considered YouTube as a way to market their art. Towards the end of 2016, they uploaded their first video. Three years of hard work and eighty-five videos later, they had gained a large fan following. Over time, Team Naach has grown from one location to seven in Mumbai, and now teaches around 5,000 students.

STAY OUT OF YOUR COMFORT ZONE

Success happens when preparation meets opportunity. If you are not prepared when opportunity knocks, then you cannot grow. Never mind how successful you are, if you are ambitious, do not get into a comfort zone. Keep preparing, keep sweating, because opportunities come as surprises.

Team Naach began posting videos online so that more people would get to know about them and more students would join their classes. But YouTube opened many other doors for them. The duo started posting dance videos on trending songs with simpler moves. People searching for trending songs made these videos visible. After three videos, there was a spike in the channel subscriber base. Certain aggregators also began sharing Team Naach's videos and within three months, there was considerable traction. Nicole says, 'Due to the copyright limitations by music labels, we could not monetise our videos.

So there was no advertising revenue coming from YouTube. But we kept posting videos to build a brand.'

One day, Nicole's friend Ajith sent her a video of the song 'Jimikki Kammal' (from the Malayalam film *Velipadinte Pusthakam*), telling her it was a viral song and Team Naach should choreograph it. Nicole and Sonal liked the song very much and shot the video on Sonal's mobile phone. That YouTube video went viral and was even covered by a regional TV channel. Because of this video, the girls were noticed by Malayalam film producer Vijay Babu, and got a dance opportunity for the song 'Changaathi Nannayal' in the Malayalam film *Aadu 2*.

These two songs established Team Naach in the south and led to the YouTube FanFest performance opportunity in both Chennai and Bangalore. The audience at the FanFest asked them for a workshop, and close to 500 people participated. This experiment led to the new idea of doing workshops in different cities. Team Naach created partners in various cities and, with their help, started organising workshops. These workshops helped Team Naach build a personal connection with thousands of dance enthusiasts pan India.

Starting from 2018, Team Naach has performed at many YouTube FanFests. There, the girls met many other top YouTubers of India and came up with collaboration ideas. A few, such as Bhuvan Bam and Prajakta Koli, have performed with Nicole and Sonal in the videos. Nicole says, 'The demand curve suddenly went on a surge. People started asking for more videos on our channel. Brands started approaching for placement, fashion designers started asking us to try their costumes and even music labels started asking us to choreograph their songs.' To meet the demand, Team Naach increased their video posting frequency from one video a month to three to four videos a month. Nicole says, 'The channel subscriber growth from 1 to

2 million was pretty quick. However, the growth from 2 to 3 million was slow. This was when we increased the number of experiments.' The duo tried fusion of different dance styles, and also started tutorials and quizzes. They involved subscribers by asking them to replicate the dances they liked and to post them on social media. The growth of subscribers from 3 to 4 million happened rapidly.

The choreography industry is getting more and more fast-paced. Dancing is a profession where trends keep changing, and one has to keep learning to be future-ready. Earlier, Team Naach had sufficient time to rehearse, but to meet the increased demand, the rehearsal time has reduced drastically. Also, because of their popularity, people's expectations have also risen. Nicole says, 'Because you're never going to have unlimited time, you can't beat yourself up when things are not perfect. At the same time, you have to honour the expectations of your audience consistently.' Sonal adds, 'If I fail, I am okay. But if I don't try, then I have a problem. So, we had to draw a line somewhere.'

Nicole and Sonal have different personalities. Nicole is outgoing and organised. She is very good at planning and strategising. She says, 'Sometimes I overthink. I have learnt from Sonal to take things more lightly and be calm.' Sonal, in turn says, 'We are different and have found a way to work with each other. Also, we have gained a lot from each other's strengths. Nicole prepares the list of tasks to be done and makes sure that we complete them on time.' They keep pushing each other to stay out of their comfort zone.

TEAMWORK MAXIMISES THE CHANCES OF WINNING

In Maharashtra, the festival of Janmashtami is celebrated with the Dahi Handi. The event involves making a human pyramid and breaking an earthen pot, hung at a certain height and filled with milk, curd, butter, fruit and water. The term 'Govinda' refers to those who form the human pyramid. Not all Govindas are alike. Based on their body types, they play different roles. Some are athletic and can climb. Some are strong. They create the base for the pyramid and carry the load of the others. While everyone looks at the Govinda climbing to the top, usually a young boy, the pyramid is only possible because of the Govindas who stay on the ground and allow others to climb on their shoulders. The team wins due to the combined effort. The Govinda climbing to the top feels confident because he has the support of the many Govindas below.

Similarly, Sonal and Nicole are able to showcase a lot of creativity and confidence in front of their audience because of the team that supports them behind the scenes. It might occur to you to ask that if Sonal and Nicole are ace choreographers and dancers, why do they need the support of a team? Well, the process of creating dance videos has much more to it than dance. Let's look at some of the complexities.

The organisation of different dance phrases creates the entire dance, conveying a particular idea. Usually, different dance phrases include short pauses or powerful body moves. The intricacy of the dance phrase is determined by the dance movements it is made up of. Each movement has to flow easily and naturally into another within the phrase, without awkward transitions. To help communicate the dramatic content, dance movements are often enhanced by other visual elements such as costume, music, make-up, lighting and acting.

Further, to create a video, choreographers must understand camera angles, lighting and different lenses. They also must know which movements work best for a wide shot and what looks great in slow motion. The location of a dance has an important effect on the way movement is perceived. A small space can make the movement look outstanding, while a large area can make the same movement appear insignificant. The reality is that a choreographer is taxed both mentally and physically.

The biggest problem with creating online content is to come up with something original every time. But many brains are better than just one, so when Team Naach brainstorms and shares ideas, the sky is the limit. Sonal says, 'What works for us is that we have a team that assembles the ideas, and then we brainstorm.' Today, Team Naach has a great team. But it took Nicole and Sonal many trials and misses to find the right members. Nicole says, 'We made our hiring mistakes and learnt from them. Eventually, we created the team we are proud of.'

IN CONCLUSION

Fashion world legend Ralph Lauren started his journey as a tie salesman and created one of the world's biggest fashion empires. He once said, 'I didn't have a vision as in, this is where I'm going. I had a vision as in, this is what I love to do.' Along the same lines, when Nicole and Sonal started their small dance class, they didn't know where they would reach. They just loved what they did. By following their passion, within a few years, the duo has come a long way. Today, when they walk on the road, people recognise them because of their work, not because of their jobs or fancy titles.

Perspectives from Sonal Devraj and Nicole Concessao

- When you have an unconventional career, don't be bothered by what people say. Follow your dream. If you are consistent and put your 100 per cent, something good will happen.
- Even if you reach a certain point of success, keep your passion the same as when you started your journey. Always think about what you can do better and put in as much effort as you can.
- You cannot do all the things. It's good to create a team and work with people with whom you can get along.
- People are different. If you are working with someone, respect the other person and their ideas. Also, respect their personal space.
- Set small goals at the start. Achieving them will give you confidence to achieve bigger goals later.

YASHRAJ MUKHATE

YASHRAJ MUKHATE

From Engineer to Popular Music Composer

Whether you think you can, or you think you can't, you're right.

—Henry Ford

Have you heard the story of the balloon seller and the little boy? It bears retelling: There was once a balloon seller who sold helium–filled balloons near a children's park. One day, out of curiosity, a young boy asked the seller, 'Will a black balloon reach the same height as a red, yellow or any other bright colour balloon?' The seller smiled and said, 'Let me show you how high this black balloon can fly.' To the boy's surprise, the black balloon reached high into the sky. Pointing a finger towards the black balloon in the sky, the seller said, 'That balloon is not flying because of its colour. It is flying because of what is inside.' The moral of the story is our mindset defines where we reach in life.

In 2012, Yashraj Mukhate was rejected at the audition for Indian Idol, the most popular singing show in India. However, he bounced back, and by 2021, at the age of twenty-five, he was one of the most popular singer-composers in the country. Though many people noticed Yashraj in 2021, his rising popularity had already started the year before. In 2020, Yashraj's mash-up 'Rasode main kaun tha?' caught the attention of many Bollywood personalities and made him an internet sensation. In 2021, his mash-up 'Pawri hori hai' crossed 64 million views in just two months and made him a household name. The same year, many other exciting things happened. National media channels such as NDTV covered Yashraj. He won the prestigious Mirchi Trendsetter of the Year award, and was included in the prestigious Grazia Cool List of 2021. Anu Malik, a judge on Indian Idol from 2004–18, welcomed him to his own home, appreciating his work. Yashraj also had the opportunity to interview his role model, legendary music composer A.R. Rahman.

As of April 2024, more than 7 million people follow Yashraj on various social media channels. Beyond being an emerging celebrity in the music world, Yashraj has become a preferred jingle creator for brands like Tata Sky, Dream 11, Wakefit and many others. He has collaborated with celebrities such as cricket star Virat Kohli, Bollywood star Ajay Devgn and famous music composer Amit Trivedi. Additionally, he has launched his own record label, YM Originals.

This is the story of Yashraj Mukhate, a musician from Aurangabad, who used the power of the internet to create a unique path for himself.

THE BEGINNING

Yashraj was born on 28 November 1995, in Aurangabad. His father, Bhushanraj Mukhate, is a real estate businessman, while his mother, Vaishali Mukhate, runs a clothing business. His elder sister, Kalyani Mukhate, went on to become an architect.

Bhushanraj Mukhate loves music and as a hobby, would perform with orchestras at local functions. Yashraj thus spent hours listening to music, right from childhood. When he was three years old, his father gifted him a musical keyboard. The keyboard fascinated him, and Yashraj began spending hours with the instrument. Seeing Yashraj's interest, his father began teaching him the basics of music. Soon, little Yashraj began to accompany his father to various events, and at the age of three, gave his first stage performance with his father. Within a few years, Yashraj was performing every week at a local church. These public performances helped boost his self-confidence.

Yashraj wanted to become a musician, but his mother wished him to be an engineer. So he decided to follow a middle path. Because of his interest in music, he considered studying sound engineering. However, he was unable to find a suitable programme, so he opted for electronics and telecommunications, as most modern musical devices have electronic parts. He did a diploma at MIT College of Engineering, Aurangabad, followed by a Bachelor of Engineering at Sinhagad College, Pune.

While in college, Yashraj also performed at birthday parties and marriage functions. This exposure not only helped to further boost his self-confidence, but also earned him some pocket money. After completing his engineering degree in 2018, he told his parents that he would like to follow his passion for music.

Steve Jobs once said, 'If you really look closely, most overnight successes took a long time.' Yashraj's journey was similar. He started his YouTube channel in 2009, and till 2018, he had only 24,000 views. But, from 2019 onwards, things changed. Now, every video he posts crosses a million views. There are many valuable lessons to be learnt from the evolution of Yashraj Mukhate as a personal brand. Here are some of them.

DON'T GIVE UP

If you thought you could do something very well, and people around you appreciated your craft, then suddenly you failed publicly, how would you feel? Devasted, certainly. But for how long? If you remained sunk in depression and disappointment, you could lose yourself and the track you were following. But if you were to stand up quickly and fight back like a sportsperson, you could change the final outcome.

Growing up, Yashraj loved listening to singers and musicians, and wanted to become one. At school, he was active in every opportunity to do with singing and playing instruments. At home, he would record his voice samples over and over again. Yashraj says ruefully, 'I was a terrible singer. But with practice, I improved.' He spent early mornings, nights and weekends practising. Eventually, he began to improve. With time, people in Aurangabad began recognising Yashraj's talent and suggested that he participate in Indian Idol.

There have been many Indian Idol contestants who went on to have successful careers in Bollywood. Yashraj's father had not been able to pursue his dream of becoming a professional musician because of the lack of suitable platforms in the past. He felt Indian Idol could be a launch pad for his son. Using his network of contacts, Bhushanraj Mukhate arranged an audition at Indian Idol.

On the day of the audition, father and son left Aurangabad at 6 a.m., filled with hope. When they reached Mumbai at 10 a.m., they found hundreds of candidates had come to audition. They also discovered that the preliminary round would be judged by the show's producers, not the judges. Having waited for 3 hours, Yashraj was called in. Before he could complete one line, he was asked to stop.

His glorious vision was shattered. His father was disappointed. Yashraj did not understand where he had gone wrong and why he had not been allowed to sing the entire song, or at least enough to show what he could do. Returning home to Aurangabad, he said to his father, 'This route is not for me. I will create my own path through the internet.'

That was 2012. There were no examples of any artist making it big without a platform like Indian Idol, and that too, through the internet. Bhushanraj Mukhate was not confident that things would turn out well, but he appreciated Yashraj's confidence and encouraged him saying, 'Maybe something better and bigger is waiting for you!'

STUDY YOUR HEROES

Legendary investor Warren Buffet once said, 'If you tell me who your heroes are, I'll tell you how you're gonna turn out.' Role models or heroes are necessary for self-improvement. They influence our actions and motivate us to reveal our true potential and conquer our weaknesses. This was so for Yashraj as well. By following his role models, Yashraj has worked on his craft for thousands of hours and improved enormously.

Today, music composers come from various backgrounds. Some have master's degrees in film music, while others have never taken a formal course. Yashraj belongs to the latter category. He says, 'There's no right or wrong way to start your journey. There's no perfect background, upbringing or education that makes a great music composer. You will suffer your own setbacks and disappointments, and you'll achieve your own successes and triumphs. What will make you great are your role models, your dedication in following them and the practice you put into becoming an artist.' Among Yashraj's role models are Amit

Trivedi and A.R. Rahman. When he listens to their songs, he tries to understand how they play their notes and the emotion in their performance.

Developing a musical approach to a film scene involves multiple considerations, such as the physical surroundings and environment, a character's personality, thoughts and feelings at that moment, and so on. To understand all these aspects, Yashraj watches film songs many times. If, for any reason, the scene gets reordered, then the music composer faces the task of substantially altering the structure of his music. It's never easy to reorder existing music to play with reordered scenes. To understand the approaches of famous music composers, Yashraj listens to their interviews and notes down their strategies.

He says, 'I noticed Amit Trivedi's work in *Dev.D.* Since then, I have found his every small or big, popular or underrated work, and studied it as deeply as I can. He is amazing!' A.R. Rahman has been an inspiration to Amit Trivedi right from the beginning. Yashraj noticed the name of A.R. Rahman when he listened to the songs of the film *Jaane Tu... Ya Jaane Na*. In the course of his research, he found that A.R. Rahman was the music director of popular films like *Roja* and *Dil Se*. Yashraj says, 'A.R. Rahman's portfolio is vast. I would need a lifetime to study it properly. I worship him like God.' When it comes to music, A.R. Rahman has often expressed his appreciation for Ilaiyaraaja, so, Yashraj too, studied the work of Ilaiyaraaja.

Music is produced in beats, bars and phrases. A bar is a group of beats, and a phrase is a group of bars. One of Yashraj's techniques for practising is to dismantle a piece of music and put it back together. Every day, he spends several hours studying and dissecting components of music that has caught his ear. He listens carefully to his own creation for imperfections, the effect of various musical instruments, background noises, mouth sounds, pitch inaccuracies, etc. 'Every day is filled with trials and errors. If I am unhappy with the outcome, I keep on reworking till I am satisfied,' Yashraj says. With complete dedication, Yashraj has also recreated the music of many famous musicians with a variety of instruments.

TO CONNECT THE DOTS, FIRST COLLECT THE DOTS

After Steve Jobs' speech at Stanford University, 'connect the dots' became a famous phrase. But, to connect the dots you have to first collect the dots. The rise in digital content has made YouTube a crowded place. When there are so many creators, there are multiple videos on similar topics. This vast content is also the repository of a vast number of ideas or dots, which could be connected in various forms and shapes to create something new and unheard of.

One of the approaches that has helped Yashraj is consuming a lot of content. He says, 'The more content I consume, the more ideas I get.' He listens to regional music, musicians of different generations and musicians of other countries. He got the idea of making meme songs from Dub Sharma, known for his work in the Bollywood film *Gully Boy*. He got many ideas from a music-based MTV mini-series called *Sound Trippin*, hosted by Sneha Khanwalkar. In this show, she travels to places like Punjab, Banaras, Goa and Leh, collecting sounds of local singers and musicians and creating a final piece of music that resonates with the feel and sounds of that location.

By watching the videos of an Iranian musician, Yashraj learnt a cappella, a musical voice form that has no instrumental accompaniment. His a cappella performance on a *Baahubali* song using a broom and water tank became very popular on the internet. Yashraj says, 'Learn from others, but don't try to copy them. Create your own style. Don't follow something that is in trend, because 100 more people are thinking in that direction. To stand out, you need to bring exclusivity in your work.'

With the internet penetrating small towns and villages, it is often difficult to balance what a creator wants to create and what his audience wants to watch. Yashraj suggests focusing on something niche, liked by a small audience. He believes that if a small audience loves your work, they then bring more people to your channel. At the same time, he loves experimenting. So, along with his proven and trending work, he posts experiments and gauges audience response once in a while. Yashraj says, 'Everyone has to experiment as there is no progress without experimentation. I have heard that A.R. Rahman has two rooms. In one room, he practises with tried and tested technology, and in the other one, he experiments with new technology.'

Yashraj's discipline has made him one of the most popular music creators in India, and consequently, his fan base has kept growing. He is devoted to his audience and says, 'Whatever I have achieved is because of my audience. I never take them for granted.' He interacts directly with his audience online by responding to their comments. Besides, he makes sure he is giving his audience quality content. Initially, he tried following a weekly video upload schedule, but found that the forced consistency was compromising quality. So he decided to post only when he was satisfied with the content. Yashraj says, 'It's not easy to always come up with fresh content that will be liked by the masses. I understand that every video I put out will not go viral.'

Sometimes, Yashraj gets interesting ideas quickly, and sometimes, even after trying for days and weeks, nothing comes. While creative people cannot pinpoint why great ideas often come to them at unexpected places and unusual times, there's definitely something to letting your brain relax. When Yashraj gets stuck, he forces himself to keep going. But in the absence of expected progress, he takes a nap or goes for a walk. When you relax, your mind subconsciously organises thoughts and memories, and you may find that an idea that seemed entirely out of your grasp suddenly comes into focus after a rest. Yashraj says, 'Many ideas have clicked with me unexpectedly while taking a shower or watching TV! And I always look forward to such eureka moments.'

IF YOU DON'T FIND A PATH, CREATE IT

Just because a visible path does not exist, or we do not have experience of it from the past, or others say it cannot be done, it does not mean the thing cannot be done. Sometimes, the thrill of trying something new, a positive attitude and self-confidence can create paths that change your life. Something similar happened to Yashraj.

Salim Merchant, a former judge of Indian Idol and a famous music composer known for his work in films like *Chak De India*, posted a contest on social media. Yashraj applied. Salim shared Yashraj's video in his Instagram stories. Yashraj messaged him with a request for a meeting though he did not expect a response. To his surprise, Salim agreed to meet that Sunday at his studio in Mumbai. When Yashraj met Salim, he told the famous composer about the challenges he faced in composing music. Salim asked him, 'Do you know how to swim?' Yashraj replied, 'Yes, very well!' Then Salim asked him, 'Were you a good swimmer from day one?' To which Yashraj replied, 'No, I became a good swimmer with practice.' Salim suggested he follow the same approach in music composition.

Since then, Yashraj has been in touch with Salim through WhatsApp, sharing his work. He says, 'Salim usually responds after looking at my work. But whenever I don't get a response, I get a feeling that he has not liked my work and I have to improve.'

As Yashraj lives in Aurangabad, he does not have the luxury of visiting shows and events in Mumbai. So he figured out an interesting approach to connect with artists. He began creating covers of famous songs, and while posting these on social media, he tagged all the artists mentioned in the credit section of the video's description on YouTube. This approach helped him to get noticed by various influential musicians and Bollywood personalities. Yashraj recalls, 'Surprisingly, icons like Vishal Dadlani, A.R. Rahman, Anu Malik and Amit Trivedi noticed my work, as I had tagged them.'

In August 2020, Yashraj uploaded a 57-second video of him remixing a light-hearted line of dialogue from the Hindi TV serial *Saath Nibhaana Saathiyaa*. This mash-up 'Rasode mein kaun tha?' got almost 10 million views within a week. When he uploaded this video, he had 24,000 followers on Instagram and roughly 8,000 subscribers on YouTube. In less than a week, these numbers crossed the 600,000 mark on both platforms. The video was shared by the likes of singer Prateek Kuhad and actors Rajkummar Rao, Taapsee Pannu and Varun Dhawan. As a pleasant surprise, Yashraj received a message from Bollywood director Anurag Kashyap, to say he had checked out Yashraj's work. Anurag shared his number and said, 'Let's connect'.

Yashraj is a big fan of Anurag Kashyap. His films like *Black Friday*, *Dev.D* and *Gangs of Wasseypur* have been on his favourites list. For the next two days, he could not sleep, waiting to meet Anurag. As soon as the COVID-19 lockdown eased, Yashraj travelled to Mumbai to meet Anurag. Yashraj shared his new work with him. Anurag asked Yashraj about his role models. When Yashraj mentioned Amit Trivedi, Anurag immediately called Amit and scheduled a meeting with him that same day. Yashraj says, 'It was Teachers' Day. Meeting two of the icons of Bollywood, whom I consider my teachers, on this auspicious day, was a godsent opportunity for me.'

In March 2021, around the festival of Holi, Yashraj messaged Anu Malik, requesting him for a meeting. To his surprise, Anu Malik responded and welcomed him warmly to his home. During this meeting, Yashraj told him, 'Ten years ago, I didn't get a chance to see you, as I was rejected in the Indian Idol audition. Today, I consider myself fortunate to meet you.' Appreciating Yashraj's journey, Anu Malik said, 'Everything happens for a reason. If you had not been rejected, you might not have discovered your unique path.'

After meeting Anu Malik, Yashraj called famous stand-up comedian Zakir Khan and asked him for a meeting. Zakir had noticed Yashraj's work, so he happily agreed to meet for dinner. Over dinner, Zakir guided Yashraj on how to handle brand deals and grow as an artist.

That same month, Yashraj heard that A.R. Rahman was visiting Mumbai to promote the film *99 Songs*. Yashraj created a cover of one of the songs from the film and tagged A.R. Rahman and his team on social media. Then he messaged the film team for an opportunity to interview A.R. Rahman. They agreed!

Yashraj says, 'If you follow a crowded path, then you have to be exceptionally talented to surpass the competition. On the other hand, the internet allows you to put your work in the public domain. You never know; some of your work might go viral and bring you surprises you had never expected.'

ENJOY SHORT-TERM SUCCESS, BUT DON'T LOSE LONG-TERM FOCUS

American football player Curtis Martin once said, 'Never let a short-term desire get in the way of a long-term goal'. When people become successful, it is natural for them to become inclined towards their short-term desires, while ignoring their long-term goals. However, if one remains focused, one keeps preparing for the future. If you look closely, you will find that artists who stay relevant in the long run do not get into the comfort zone with short-term achievements.

At a very young age, Yashraj received a lot of attention due to his viral mash-ups. He says, 'I knew short content always works as Instagram is all about short content. But I didn't know that my short videos would become so big. But this was not my ultimate aim. I wanted people to hear my music, which I attached to the dialogues.' He knows that these meme or mash-up videos attract audiences, so he has to create them. But he also knows that this trending content has a short shelf life. To build a long-term career, he has to compose complete songs.

Composing involves a high degree of uncertainty. A musician starts most of his projects with no idea what the finished score will sound like. As a composer, he would like to think that inspiration will strike quickly. But writing something memorable does not happen often. Typically, a composer has to sit down with musical instruments and experiment with notes and sounds until he discovers something he can develop. Yashraj says, 'Every time I do something out of my comfort zone, I doubt whether I will be able to do it. But this doubt also helps me navigate things better.'

When Yashraj is tied to a production schedule for a brand jingle or a television show, he has to generate ideas immediately.

He says, 'When brands were not there, I used to work at my own pace and get a lot of creative satisfaction. Now, I have deadlines. Also, I have to keep reporting to brands on my progress, which is uncertain in the creative world.' To adapt to the demanding situation, Yashraj thinks practice is the only solution. Even when he doesn't have a deadline, he challenges himself to develop a theme or melody on a strict timeline. He likes to see what he can produce when he gives himself only one, two or three weeks to create something. Yashraj says, 'Often, nothing happens for the whole day, and I have to go to sleep restless.'

It can be emotionally exhausting to continue a musical journey without support and feedback from the audience. Therefore, growing musicians simply cannot restrict their work to themselves. They need to publish their work through social media and other fora. Artists may receive criticism of their work, but they cannot let criticism take over. They need to work on their skills constantly. There is no substitute for practice.

Yashraj says, 'My meme videos bring the audience to my channel. There, the audience explores my other work, and I get to know their feedback.' However, he is careful about what he presents to his audience. He believes one bad piece can stop audiences from returning. So, he focuses on quality work over quantity. On his computer, the folder of his deleted work is ten times larger than the folder of his published work.

IN CONCLUSION

Paulo Coelho's masterpiece, *The Alchemist*, tells the mystical story of Santiago, a shepherd boy who desires to travel in search of a worldly treasure. His quest leads him to riches far different and far more satisfying than he ever imagined. The story represents the transforming power of our dreams, the people in our lives, and the importance of listening to our heart.

In similar fashion, when Yashraj began his journey, he could not imagine that the universe had its own plans for him. Today, he is an inspiration for every small-town child who wants to make it big in life, and has one thing—access to the internet.

Perspectives from Yashraj Mukhate

- Do not copy anyone else's style. Be authentic. People like authenticity.
- According to the Law of Attraction, you attract into your life whatever you think about. Similarly, on YouTube, you attract content similar to what you watch. If you have gone to YouTube to find something, then don't lose your focus. If you start watching some other content, you may get into the algorithm trap and waste precious time watching something you never intended to.
- If you want to stand out in your field, make those things available that are not available in the market.
- Along with studies, pursue a hobby. If you nurture your hobby, you will never lose confidence, even if you are not doing well at your studies.

ABHI AND NIYU

ABHI AND NIYU

From Video Bloggers to Change Makers

You may never know what results come of your actions, but if you do nothing, there will be no results.

—Mahatma Gandhi

Travelling is remarkable in so many ways. It provides a fantastic opportunity to learn, meet new people and enjoy local cuisines and cultures. Sometimes, it takes you on a journey you could never have imagined or experienced before. Columbus discovered America, Vasco da Gama discovered the sea route from Europe to Asia, and Charles Darwin formulated the theory of evolution, because they travelled. In a similar way, travel has played an essential role in the life of Abhi and Niyu.

In 2019, the husband-wife duo, Abhiraj Rajadhyaksha (Abhi) and Niyati Mavinkurve (Niyu), decided to take a 200-day break from their routine life and explore India. Their idea was to encourage social good in India by finding positive stories in places where people do not think to find any. The outcome was a breakout video series, *100 Reasons to Love India*. The series presented positive stories about India, its change makers and its history and culture, and it created an army of people working to find solutions to everyday problems. Because of this video series, within a year, the couple gained over 1.3 million subscribers on YouTube and over 1.7 million followers on Instagram.

After this series, with the continued objective of spreading positivity, the couple began making solution-oriented videos on India's pressing issues in a millennial-friendly format. Their videos span genres like history, environment, policy, social issues, economics and personal finance.

In 2021, *Forbes India* included the couple in its prestigious 30 Under 30 list, and Facebook showcased them in its hoardings across the country. This is the inspiring story of a married couple who joined hands to achieve a common dream. In 2023, the couple became the Exclusive Goodwill Ambassadors for Special Olympics Bharat to create awareness about the special athletes representing the country at the World Summer Games in Berlin, Germany. Additionally, in 2023, they were recognised as GQ's Most Influential Young Indians. In 2024, Abhi and Niyu were proud recipients of the 'New India Campaign' award from Prime Minister Narendra Modi at the National Creators Award. As of April 2024, over 8 million people follow Abhi and Niyu on various social media platforms.

THE BEGINNING

Abhi and Niyu both came from humble backgrounds. Abhi was born on 6 September 1993, in Mumbai. His parents are creative people. His father, Abhay Rajadhyaksha, directed TV serials and films, but is now in event management. His mother, Anuradha Rajadhyaksha, has been an actress in the Marathi film industry.

Till Class X, Abhi studied in a Marathi medium school. British rule, combined with the universal advantage of knowing English, has made English the preferred medium of education. This demarcation often causes an inferiority complex in students from vernacular medium schools. Abhi was fortunate to come under the guidance of one of his school teachers, Minal Paranjape, who took a keen interest in preparing vernacular medium students with conversational English skills. Abhi credits her for developing his English language skills.

In junior college, Abhi pursued commerce at NM College, Mumbai, followed by a bachelor's degree in mass media, specialising in advertising, from RD National College, Mumbai. He also did a diploma in cinematography and editing from FX School, Mumbai.

Three years older than Abhi, Niyu too, was born in Mumbai, on 18 December 1990. Her father, Anil Mavinkurve, is the managing director of JM Financial Services, and her mother, Archana Mavinkurve, worked with Castrol. Niyu studied at Bombay Cambridge School, considered one of the best schools in Mumbai. For her overall development, her parents encouraged her to join elocution and extempore speaking classes and participate in competitions. Niyu went on to do a bachelor's in commerce from NM College, Mumbai, before qualifying as a chartered accountant.

In 2010, both were in NM College, Mumbai, Abhi in the second year of Junior College, and Niyu in the final year of B.Com. As luck would have it, they met during Rotofest, the annual festival of the Rotaract Club of NM College. Abhi was performing, and Niyu was organising. Working together for the event gave them a chance to get to know each other. Due to the difference in their ages and the prevailing social norms, it was difficult to convince their parents. But finally, in May 2018, the two were married, with parental blessings. A year into the marriage, the couple decided to have a baby. But their baby was different. It was a brainchild—a passion project to discover India like never before.

There are many valuable lessons to be learnt from the evolution of Abhi and Niyu as a brand. We share a few of them here.

STRIVE TO REACH OUT TO PEOPLE

Networking is one of the most important business/life skills you will ever learn. Many people think networking is about exchanging business cards at a conference. This is not correct. Networking is about identifying the right people, striving to reach out to them and finding ways to add value to them. It means having to think hard about what others need and what you can offer. This process could be time-consuming, but it is exciting and enriching. When you care about others, they are likely to care about you in turn.

In their journey, Abhi and Niyu have tried to connect with others by offering some value, and the payoffs have been huge. Since January 2017, Abhi has been following Nas Daily (Nuseir Yassin), a Harvard graduate who quit his job as a software engineer to record his world travel experiences. In the process, he created 1,000 daily 1-minute videos and posted them on Facebook. Consequently, he became one of the world's most popular social media influencers. In August 2017, Nas ran a contest to work with global content creators. It was the first time Abhi made short and crisp videos, which got Nas' attention. Abhi met Nas at his Mumbai meet-up and offered to help him in whatever way he could. He accompanied Nas as a translator on his trip to Dharavi. Nas got a perspective about India, and Abhi was able to look at Nas' content creation journey up close.

To experience Indian culture and expose his followers to an Indian wedding, Nas planned a fake wedding ceremony at a farmhouse in Panvel, a Mumbai suburb. Abhi helped him to create a film. When Nas reached Delhi, he called Abhi to ask, 'Can you join me here? I think you can help me in navigating many things in India.' Abhi took the chance.

While travelling with Nas across Delhi, Abhi discussed many subjects, including the future of travel content. He showed Nas a YouTube video series, *Way Back Home*, created by Rohan Thakur (Ronnie) and Bharati Bahrani (Barty). Nas liked it very much. Abhi asked Nas about the thing that puzzled him, 'I love this series, but I can't understand why it doesn't have as many views as your videos.' Nas shared a few valuable lessons with Abhi, such as keeping the videos short and crisp, adding subtitles and maintaining consistency in posting videos. Today, the audience likes snackable content. Subtitles set context, and frequency helps to keep the audience engaged. These valuable lessons helped Abhi when he launched his *Following Love* initiative on Facebook in December 2017.

Like Abhi, Niyu has also achieved much through value-based networking. She decided to collaborate with brands on their honeymoon trip to Austria and Germany. She approached various tourism boards in these countries. Her pitch was that as a couple, she and Abhi could create tourism promotion videos for them. Austria's Innsbruck Tourism Board suggested she approach their collaboration partner in India—Ishvinder Maddh, MD of Robinville Intech. He liked Abhi's video on Udaipur and helped the couple plan an itinerary with Innsbruck Tourism. In this way, Abhi and Niyu unwittingly experienced their first press trip, and it all started because of the chance Niyu took to reach out to tourism boards because she believed in the content Abhi created.

DON'T COMPARE YOUR START WITH SOMEONE ELSE'S PRESENT

Everybody loves a beautiful butterfly. But a butterfly is not born flying in beauty. It begins life as a small egg. When the egg hatches, a little caterpillar emerges. The caterpillar goes through a developmental process within a cocoon. Eventually, from the cocoon emerges a beautiful butterfly with wings. A popular celebrity is like a beautiful butterfly, flying and visible to everyone.

On social media, when aspiring creators look at popular creators' lives, they are convinced the other person is happier, healthier and wealthier. They tend to romanticise and believe they too can have a similar life if they get into the same profession. Sadly, they miss out on a crucial part—that they are seeing a creator when they have become popular, not when they were struggling and working hard to stand out. Rather than staying focused on someone's good fortune, zoom out and look at their developmental process, their days of being a caterpillar.

Niyu says, 'A lot of hard work goes behind the scenes, which a creator does not share with their audience.' Working while travelling is not half as attractive as it sounds. There were times when Abhi spent the whole day in video editing and Niyu in writing. Abhi says, 'We didn't travel for fun. We travelled for a purpose. We were constantly being evaluated for our videos, and there was definitely a lot of pressure.' In the course of their journey, the couple worked in buses, airplanes and airports. Niyu says, 'The journey of becoming a known content creator needs a lot of patience.' The couple's video content is backed by numbers, data and a lot of research. There have also been times when, despite reading hundreds of articles, they could not create a video.

Many aspiring and new content creators do not move ahead because of nervousness and self-doubt. They imagine self-doubt exists only in them, and not in the bigger creators who appear confident in their videos. Abhi says, 'I don't think any person in the creative field has not faced self-doubt. It's the part of the process that pushes you to keep improving your craft. Because the day you feel you know everything, your downfall begins.' There is one other myth. Seeing the lifestyles of bigger creators, people imagine there is constant and steady income in this field. Abhi sets this right by saying, 'Some months, you earn a lot, and some months there is no income. Sometimes, you invest a lot of time and money in an idea, and nothing comes of it. If you are looking for stability and consistency, then the creative field is not for you.'

Many new creators reach out to established creators with collaboration requests, given their followers. Niyu says, 'It is fine to reach out to bigger creators for collaboration, but one should be clear what collaboration means. It means both parties bring something to the table, so that there is an exchange of ideas. If you are reaching out to a bigger creator, be clear about your value proposition. The big creator is bringing his millions of followers. What are you bringing to match that value?'

The bigger creators receive numerous requests from newcomers to share their videos or appear in their videos. These are favours, not collaborations. A new creator must respect the time and effort a bigger creator has put in to reach where they are today. Ideally, a new creator should put in most of the effort in such a collaboration because they have yet to prove themselves, while an established creator brings reputation and reach to the table.

In 2018, Nas revisited India and invited Abhi and Niyu to a Facebook conference he was attending. Here, the couple got a chance to meet chef and internet personality, Sanjyot Keer. At the time, Abhi and Niyu were unknown in the digital world, and Sanjyot was a star. But he humbly listened to their ideas and agreed to collaborate on a video for his Facebook page, *Your Food Lab*. For this opportunity, Abhi and Niyu worked very hard on scripting, the video shoot and editing. The video got 500,000 views within hours, and the couple earned their first advertising revenue from Facebook, worth ₹6,000.

The video got views because of the popularity of the *Your Food Lab* page and Sanjyot's presence in the video. But Sanjyot deeply appreciated the couple's hard work behind the scenes. Abhi says, 'If you want to benefit from another person's influence, you have to think about the hard work you can do to add value. This makes the outcome better.'

EXPERIENCE THE JOURNEY, DON'T WORRY ABOUT THE DESTINATION

Late tennis player Arthur Ashe once said, 'Success is a journey, not a destination. The doing is often more important than the outcome.' If you think too much about the destination, you tend to imagine the future instead of focusing on what you can achieve in the present. If you shift your focus from the destination to the journey, your mindset changes entirely; you focus on today's tasks. You learn and grow in the journeying. Reaching the destination is just a consequence of your journey.

Niyu started her finance career with a start-up, but the work–life balance was unsatisfactory. So she quit within six months to figure out her life. She began taking on freelance writing assignments. Between 2014–19, Abhi made videos for agencies and brands, and earned significant experience in making different types of films. But he also felt dissatisfied as he was ultimately doing projects for others and amplifying their voices. He had no creative outlet to put forth his own thoughts.

Meeting Nas in 2017 changed a lot of things for Abhi. He realised that, like Nas, he could try something for himself. And so, in December 2017, he took a leap of faith and started *Following Love* on Facebook. He originally intended to make videos like *Humans of New York*.

His idea was to ask people their definition of love and he would create short videos based on their answers. However, he got short, ambiguous or random answers. Abhi says, 'In hindsight, that idea failed on the first day. People aren't comfortable talking about topics like this, especially when someone asks them upfront.' To accommodate the *Following Love* project with his regular freelance job, Abhi decided to travel once a month, to capture stories and post weekly videos. Between November 2017 and March 2018, he travelled to Udaipur, Dharamshala, Chikmagalur and across Mumbai. He created a series of twelve videos for Season 1. Abhi says, 'Twelve videos were not sufficient to decide success or failure, so I decided to continue making videos.'

After their marriage in May 2018, Abhi told Niyu he wanted her to appear with him in the videos. Niyu reluctantly agreed. They made informative videos about the places they visited in Austria, giving the beautiful locations a historical context. They also made informative videos about navigating public transport and exploring new areas and shared travel tips. But these videos did not find much traction outside their own circle.

Unsure about the whole content creation journey and discouraged by the small number of views, Abhi decided to explore foreign education. He thought they could perhaps study abroad, experience student life and work in a foreign country to build a corpus that would help them travel the world. But a trip to Matrimandir, an edifice of spiritual significance in Auroville, made Abhi realise he should look at his own country to create content. In 2019, the couple travelled to Rishikesh and experienced the divine Ganga *aarti*. There, amidst the chanting, the peaceful Ganga and the twinkling lamps, Abhi felt a profound sense of peace and a sense of direction. A few months later, the idea for the video series *100 Reasons to Love India* was born.

Abhi considered taking an eight-month break from his regular work to travel for 200 days, to explore India's hidden beauty. However, he was concerned about travel expenses and an ongoing home loan EMI. But Niyu pushed him to focus on his idea. She assured him that she would take care of the rest. The couple started their travels in May 2019. Simultaneously, to fund the trip, Niyu continued with her writing projects.

When they started this journey, Abhi and Niyu had no roadmap and no idea what they would cover. All they knew was that they would begin each video with the line 'Did you know?' and end with 'And that's the reason why I love India'. Abhi firmly believes in the lesson from the *Bhagavad Gita*: work without thinking about the reward. As a worst-case scenario, the couple thought that even if no one watched their videos, they would have a collection of 100 videos for which they had given their absolute best. They knew the memories of this journey would last forever and become part of their life journey.

Because they started with a clear goal and an open mind, many doors opened to them in the course of their travels, things they could not have foreseen or planned for.

CURIOSITY IS KEY TO LEARNING NEW THINGS

Curiosity is an essential element of professional growth. It makes learning more effective and enjoyable. Curious people not only ask questions but actively seek out answers. It was Abhi and Niyu's curiosity to know about India that took them to many uncommon places. To satisfy their curiosity, they looked at things from both the bird's eye view and the worm's view. Here, 'bird's eye view' refers to the macro perspective, involving internet research, while 'worm's view' means looking at a particular area profoundly and thoroughly, and involves discussions with other people.

During the initial period of their journey, the couple visited places based on their research and reading. In Unakoti, Tripura, they learnt about its unique sculptures, which had been carved directly on rocks formed between the seventh and tenth centuries. In the deep jungles of Mundgod, Karnataka, they met people of the Siddi tribe, a group of African-origin Indians, who had been brought to India about 400 years ago by the Portuguese. They also visited the Chinese Kali Temple in Kolkata, where noodles are served as prasad.

As their schedule was very tight, the couple jumped from research and travel for one video, to that required for the next. To save costs and increase the number of places visited, they made travel decisions based on two factors—the fare and the weather at the location. Once they had decided on a location, they found the best way to travel to it, whether by air, road or rail. They relied almost entirely on state transport buses for inter-city travel, and once, when they could not get a shared taxi in Tripura, they even hitched a ride in a truck. The couple was also conscious of where to spend and where to save. They saved money on food by eating at small dhabas and roadside eateries rather than bigger restaurants. This contributed much to their knowledge of local cuisines. But, to safeguard their expensive equipment, they avoided staying at risky places and chose safe hotels instead, even if they were more expensive. They saved their funds by choosing to travel by bus instead of taking private taxis.

During this journey, the couple had many arguments because of stress and disagreements about various things. But they gave more importance to the regularity of their videos. To mitigate the risk of longer fights, the couple stuck to a simple rule—that any argument would be closed before they slept, even if they had to stay awake till 3 a.m. to sort out the matter. Usually, aware of the pressure of the next day's travel, they sorted their issues quickly and went to sleep on time.

Sometimes, they went to places for certain kinds of stories. The locals told them many things they would never have found in their research. For instance, they went to shoot the famous boat race in Aranmula in Pathanamthitta, Kerala. The locals told them Aranmula was also known for its metal alloy mirrors. The artisans polish metals so well that you can see your reflection in them. One of their most expensive mirrors cost ₹5 lakh. Similarly, they heard about a family in Gujarat that designs the *Patan Patola*, an expensive double ikat fabric. A single saree costs ₹2 lakh and takes ten months to create.

As travelling content creators, the internet was essential to Abhi and Niyu. But they did travel to many remote destinations where internet connectivity was either unavailable or poor. It meant making sure videos could be uploaded. This sometimes meant staying in the hotel instead of going out. In Ladakh, the internet connectivity was so bad that it took 6 hours to upload a 3-minute video. Sometimes, they even skipped beautiful destinations as they needed time to work. For instance, in Kerala, they chose not to visit the famous Athirappilly Waterfalls, shown in the movie *Baahubali*, because they were over 2 hours away from the hotel and their work was incomplete.

Over time, their followers grew and even suggested interesting places to visit or people to meet. When they were in Ladakh, they made videos about India's ice hockey team, who come from there. They also met Chewang Norphel (the Ice Man of India), who has created artificial glaciers to solve the water problem in Ladakh. In 2015, he was awarded the Padma Shri by the Government of India for his groundbreaking work that has helped countless Ladakhi villages.

Due to COVID-19, the couple's travel came to a halt. But they did not stop making videos on topics relevant to Indians. They first spend two days in extensive research about a topic. Niyu says, 'Whatever topic we choose, we research anything and everything around it. It is like creating a jigsaw puzzle and filling it with facts. For example, if we look at the second battle of Panipat, then we also look into who fought that battle, what happened before and after it, how it impacted the country and then dig deeper into the first battle and the third battle. This creates a big picture that helps broaden understanding. Then we share these facts in the form of an engaging story, along with our opinion.' Once the research is complete, the couple spends a day in scripting, one day in shooting and one day editing the video.

Niyu says, 'One should be curious in life. Unfortunately, many people expect instant returns from their knowledge, which is the wrong approach. Knowledge never goes to waste. Something that you read today might become very useful after a few years. Also, just one article or video will not give you complete information. Try to gain perspectives from multiple sources.'

USE SOCIAL MEDIA FOR SOCIAL GOOD

Using social media for social good means using it not to celebrate yourself but to change the world for the better. Hollywood actor Leonardo DiCaprio is known for his performance in movies like *Titanic* and *The Wolf of Wall Street*. He is one of the most famous celebrities in the world. As of April 2021, around 48 million people follow him on Instagram. He uses social media to create awareness about climate change and environmental issues. Because of his posts on the environment, people are becoming aware and have even taken steps to make some difference. He is a great example of someone using the power of social media for social good.

Leonardo DiCaprio has been a role model for Abhi and Niyu. Like him, they want to use the power of social media for social good. The problem they decided to focus on correcting was the perception of India. Though India has a rich culture and history, when foreigners come here and ask us what makes India special, most of us get stuck at two points—cricket and Bollywood. Sadly, when we Indians talk amongst ourselves, we discuss India's problems rather than the good things. Frequently, mainstream media and social media news feeds amplify negative news about corruption, frauds, death, sickness, crime and terrorism. When more negative news circulates in the environment than positive, people become stressed, anxious and depressed. They think India is not cool and filled with problems.

Niyu says, 'According to research by Yale University Professor Dr Laurie Santos, when you share something good and you get a reaction to it, then it actually increases your feeling of happiness. On the other hand, when you share something negative, the reaction you get does not make you feel better, and your negative feelings actually deepen.' Hence Abhi and Niyu's focus is on finding more and more positive things around India. Abhi says, 'We don't want to lecture anybody. We just want to start a conversation. Today's generation doesn't have the patience to watch a 45-minute documentary, so we decided to create 3-minute compressed videos in a millennial-friendly format.' Usually, travel bloggers just feature locations and landmarks, but Abhi and Niyu also explore history, culture and enterprising people they meet.

To reduce the negativity in the environment, the couple shares positive stories of people, companies, organisations who are doing their part to make the world a better place. Abhi says, 'We are here to tell stories of change, positivity and inspiration across India. We are here to share solutions. We are here to make India feel positive.' The couple has used Instagram reels and YouTube Shorts to talk about *Incredible India* in a series called *ABCs of Bharat*, and many reels receive over a million views regularly.

Besides sharing positive things about India, the couple has created awareness around various social causes. For instance, in 2019, the couple made a 3-minute video about the benefits of eco-friendly Ganesha idols and where to find them in Mumbai. After watching this video, people would go to a shop, show the video and say, 'We want our idol like this'. People from other cities started sharing with Abhi and Niyu details of vendors selling eco-friendly idols in their cities because they too wanted to contribute towards making the festival eco-friendly. Through social media, the eco-friendly Ganpati campaign became a nationwide campaign. Many people joined in, changing their celebrations to be more eco-friendly.

Abhi says, 'Many responses to our videos are positive, with people telling us that our videos brought them hope about the country, that we gave them new reasons to love it.' Sonam

Wangchuk, an innovator who inspired Aamir Khan's character in *3 Idiots*, noticed Abhi and Niyu when he saw their video about plastic pollution in Ladakh, explaining how to be better travellers in the mountains. He admires Abhi and Niyu's videos for their role in educating and inspiring people to make the nation, and the world, a better place.

IN CONCLUSION

American writer-producer Shonda Rhimes once said, 'You can waste your lives drawing lines. Or you can live your life crossing them.' Those who cross lines are the ones dissatisfied with the status quo, the ones who thirst for positive change. All they need is a mission, a cause to ignite them. They are the change makers.

A few years ago, Abhi and Niyu were unknown people in a crowd of millions. But their mission to spread positivity about India has given them an identity recognised by millions. Nobody gives change makers the power to change the world. They create it for themselves. That is what Abhi and Niyu did.

Perspectives from Abhi and Niyu

- If you are stuck in a monotonous routine but wish to break free, then be like Batman. Until you know it's the right time to turn your passion into your profession, pursue your full-time job in the day, like Bruce Wayne, and in your free time, become Batman and work on what your heart truly desires.
- Don't wait to achieve perfection first to start. Sometimes, it's better to start and keep getting better with time.
- Be regular. You can't expect success in the first three or five videos. Be ready to put out 50 videos, 100 videos and even 1,000 videos to achieve your dream.
- There is a misconception that the pursuit of business is to earn money. Money is like fuel. Fuel drives a car. A petrol pump is not the destination. It is just a place to get fuel so that you can reach your destination. Similarly, when you are trying to achieve some purpose, money is just a means to achieve that purpose.
- Learn before you earn. Spend your early years gaining as much experience as you can. Later, your expertise will help you to grow your career exponentially.
- When you have negative thoughts in your mind, just look down at your hands. If you don't have work, find some work to be busy with. Your mind will automatically focus on other things.

UJJWAL CHAURASIA

UJJWAL CHAURASIA

From School Student to One of India's Top Gaming YouTubers

Achievement is talent plus preparation.

—Malcolm Gladwell

Who are outliers? According to Malcolm Gladwell's book, *Outliers*, they are truly exceptional individuals who do things that are out of the ordinary. In their fields of expertise, they are so superior that they define their own category of success. Steve Jobs was an outlier, and so is Elon Musk. The incredible rise of Ujjwal Chaurasia from a government school student to one of India's youngest and biggest gaming YouTubers is truly exceptional. Given his rise at such a young age, it would not be wrong to say that he, too, is on the path to becoming an outlier.

People commonly believe that outliers are unusually gifted. However, Gladwell argues that achievement and expertise do not just happen. Rather, they result from a combination of factors such as generation, upbringing, surrounding people and an enormous amount of practice. We can see the power of these factors in Ujjwal's story.

When Ujjwal Chaurasia uploaded his first video on YouTube at the age of fifteen, he was not aware that within a short span of three years, he would become one of India's most popular gaming YouTubers. But his consistency took him to unbelievable heights. As of April 2024, almost 60 million people follow him on various social media platforms. In January 2021, he uploaded a rap song, 'Game On', that received over 23 million views in just two months. As of April 2024, the video has received over 97 million views.

This is the story of an unknown school student who is now popular in India as *Techno Gamerz*.

THE BEGINNING

Ujjwal Chaurasia was born on 12 January 2002 in a middle-class business family in Delhi. From childhood, he was a naughty and curious boy. He studied in a government school, and till Class X, along with academics, his joy came from playing outdoor games. On weekdays, he dedicated 3–5 hours every day to outdoor sports like cricket and football. And on weekends, he played for 6–7 hours. He performed quite well in both sports and academics. He was the captain of his school cricket team and one of the top-five rankers in his class.

Ujjwal was not fond of watching TV. Instead, he preferred playing mobile games. To ensure that he did not spend too much time playing games, his parents did not purchase a smartphone for him. His only option was to use his brother's phone at night, for an hour. He was so passionate about games that it was his only topic of discussion during lunch at school and dinner at home.

Ujjwal wanted to play high-end games that ran on Play Station and personal computers, but his parents would not buy these devices for him. But Ujjwal was not one to give up quickly. With his burning curiosity and passion, he discovered a way to play high-end games on his brother's smartphone. When he shared this with his friends, they thought he was bluffing, until he showed them. Ujjwal was the only person in the class who played 2 GB games on the phone when the others could only manage 100 MB games. Ujjwal became the class hero.

His friends also wanted to play such games on mobile phones, so Ujjwal shared the approach. They found it difficult to follow the suggested steps and began going to see him at home to download the games onto their phones. He could not help everyone, so he created a tutorial video with a Hindi voice-over and uploaded it on YouTube. His friends found this video very useful and asked Ujjwal to create similar tutorial videos for downloading other games he was playing. Ujjwal created seven videos before he got busy with his exams.

By the time his exams were over, these videos had received 200–300 views. Ujjwal's elder brother Ankit noticed the videos and approached Ujjwal. Ujjwal was sure he was in for a shouting, especially as he had been using Ankit's phone. But Ankit had not come to scold him. Instead, he motivated Ujjwal to become a professional YouTuber. After getting this support from his brother for his passion, Ujjwal felt very confident. He created his first YouTube channel, *Ujjwal Chaurasia*. But along with gaming videos, he began posting random videos like making Ravana for Dussehra. When Ankit discovered what Ujjwal was doing, he told him sternly not to lose focus. So, to focus on tech and gaming videos, Ujjwal created his new channel *Techno Gamerz* on 13 August 2017. Later, to focus only on live games, he started a separate YouTube channel called *Ujjwal*. Over the years, he has launched several other YouTube channels to cover content around technology and entertainment.

There are many valuable lessons to be learnt from the evolution of Ujjwal and *Techno Gamerz* as a brand. A few of them are shared here.

KEEP A BALANCE BETWEEN YOUR STUDY AND HOBBIES

There is a famous saying: do not put your feet into two boats, because if the gap between the boats widens, you can fall into deep water. As a case in point, academics is one boat, and games another. If children play games in moderation and focus on their studies too, then the gap between the two boats is not wide. But if children become obsessed with playing games, and neglect their studies, then the gap between the two boats widens, leading to adverse consequences.

Many researchers highlight that children who are involved in both sports and studies are more focused and disciplined. Ujjwal's interest in sports was as strong as his interest in academics. With his mother and brother's guidance, Ujjwal benefitted from playing sports while still having a good academic record. In order to have time to complete his homework and play sports, Ujjwal would prioritise accordingly. For example, if there was a test the next day, he would miss the afternoon's cricket practice and utilise the time to study. However, if there was an important match coming up, he would postpone his studying. The most important things he learnt from sports were focus, concentration, a competitive spirit and never giving up. These lessons aided him in his YouTube journey.

Having a controlled environment helped Ujjwal to do well academically. In Class XI, Ujjwal decided to become a computer engineer and opted for the sciences. He was surprised to find that his sports time was thus reduced from hours to minutes. Given the study load, his friends became irregular in playing after school. Not being able to play sports, Ujjwal began to feel restless.

Video games are played by over 2.6 billion people globally and have become the fastest growing form of entertainment for all age groups. India is gradually catching up with the world in terms of playing online games. In the last few years, online games have gained huge traction. Because Ujjwal loved competitive games and could play alone on a smartphone, his inclination towards video games grew stronger.

Though Ujjwal was passionate about mobile games, he did not have a smartphone. So, whenever a relative would visit, he would play on their phone. His brother Ankit, eight years his senior, worked in an animation company. At night, Ankit loaned Ujjwal his phone for an hour. Ujjwal says, 'This controlled environment helped me to keep a balance. I prepared a timetable in which I divided my day into different parts dedicated to school, coaching, outdoor games and video games. I made sure that I gave 100 per cent focus to the task in the allotted time and moved on to the next as soon as the time was over.'

BE OPEN TO DO THINGS OTHERS HAVE NOT DONE BEFORE

There is always a new way to look at the world, and new possibilities. But to do so, we have to come out of our comfort zone, think beyond traditional modes of working and consider new approaches to doing business. Ujjwal loves to figure out better ways to do things and eventually surprise the world with the results. Once, a relative gifted his mother a smartphone. Surprisingly, the phone did not have Google Play Store, so Ujjwal was unable to download mobile games on this phone. To figure out a way to download games on a smartphone without Google Play Store, Ujjwal began searching for solutions on YouTube and various blogs. After spending many sleepless nights, he found some interesting ways to download games without Play Store. He also found ways to play high-end games on a smartphone. It took Ujjwal a few more days to test his learnings and play high-end games on a low-end smartphone. Soon, his classmates realised that the games they played on a Play Station worth ₹30,000, Ujjwal played on a smartphone worth ₹5,000.

In Ujjwal's journey, his elder brother Ankit has played an important role. Ankit too, wanted to become a YouTuber, but could not do so because of his hectic work schedule. Given the family responsibilities, Ankit decided to give up his dream of becoming a YouTuber and chose to live it through his younger brother instead. Ankit was the first one to notice Ujjwal's spark and unique talent.

Reflecting on his brother's early days, Ankit says, 'Ujjwal is a quick learner, determined and hard-working. His ability to come up with innovative ideas is exemplary.' Ankit always made himself available for discussions. Ujjwal says, 'I talked a lot about video games and YouTube with my brother. I went to him every time I did something special. He would never tell me my work was exceptional or brilliant. His only reply was, "What's next?"'

When Ujjwal was in Class X, Ankit showed him a film on Steve Jobs, co-founder of Apple. He suggested Ujjwal read about his journey. Since then, Ujjwal has learnt about Steve Jobs through movies, articles and books. 'Steve Jobs was a college dropout, but that didn't stop him from finding numerous innovative products. He did things that even highly educated people didn't imagine,' Ujjwal muses. One of the things Ujjwal admires about Steve Jobs is that he created many new paths that did not exist before. He says, 'Though I have never met Steve Jobs, he is my biggest source of inspiration, thanks to my brother, who introduced me to his story. Steve Jobs' journey inspires me to create new paths for myself.'

START WITH A NICHE AND THEN EXPAND

One of the key principles Ujjwal followed at the start was to become attractive to a specific audience. He says, 'If you try to do everything, you end up doing nothing. It is better to have 100 loyal subscribers than 1,000 casual subscribers. Because loyal subscribers will share your videos and do word of mouth, which will create a pull for your channel.'

Ujjwal had started the *Techno Gamerz* channel because of his interest in technology products and gaming. But he could not talk about technology products without using them, and he did not have the resources to buy new products and creating videos. However, playing games on the phone did not require any money. So Ujjwal dropped the idea of technology product reviews and decided to focus on one niche—gaming videos. When Ujjwal started his journey, *Dragon Ball Z* was a popular game, so he thought of creating content for *Dragon Ball Z* fans. For the first few months, he focused on only on this game. He joined various groups on WhatsApp and Facebook to promote his videos. He also started adding Hindi voice-overs to his videos. Within four months he had drawn 1,000 subscribers.

By playing just one game every day for a few months, Ujjwal had got bored of it. As his passion for the game went down, so did the quality of his videos. The engagement rate on his videos began to fall. By then, *PUBG* had become a top-rated game in India. People of every age were playing it. Ujjwal too, enjoyed *PUBG*, so he thought of putting *PUBG* videos on his channel. But there was a problem. His subscribers were fans of *Dragon Ball Z*, not *PUBG*. So when he posted *PUBG* videos, the engagement rate reduced further, and followers started unsubscribing.

Ujjwal says, 'I had started with content for my audience, but now I had to shift my audience to the content that interested me.' To make this shift happen, Ujjwal came up with a strategy to post *PUBG* videos, but not to stop the *Dragon Ball Z* videos immediately. So, on alternate days, he would post two different games. That way, he was able to keep his previous audience while simultaneously attracting new ones. To achieve further growth, Ujjwal began subscribing to the top gamers on YouTube so he could watch their most popular videos. He tried to analyse what made them so popular, as well as the players' strategies. He decided to play these games differently and develop better videos than the popular ones already available on the internet. Gradually, Ujjwal began posting videos of multiple games on different days.

This strategy worked. His previous audience remained subscribed as the content they were interested in continued to appear once a week. And a new audience started coming to the channel because the content they wanted was also posted once a week. There was also a cross-pollination of interest and ideas as one audience was exposed to the game videos of the other segment.

On 6 January 2019, *Techno Gamerz* reached 100,000 subscribers. Meanwhile, Ujjwal thought of live streaming his gameplay of *PUBG* on YouTube. But he did not want to try this experiment with his existing audience on *Techno Gamerz*. So he created a separate YouTube channel, *Ujjwal*, only for live streaming. Ujjwal says, 'Live streaming is a separate niche. Creating commentary for the live stream is difficult. On the other hand, my *Techno Gamerz* channel audience enjoyed my pre-recorded videos for my commentary. I didn't want to mix these two experiences. So I created two separate channels, for the two niches.'

KEEP IMPROVING YOURSELF IN YOUR CRAFT

When you heat cold water, it takes time. At 99 degrees Celsius, water becomes very hot. At 100 degrees Celsius, water begins to boil. And boiling water becomes steam. Do you know how powerful steam is? Steam can even move a train. Too often, we give up before applying the extra one-degree effort. But if we keep pushing ourselves, we can cross the one-degree mark someday, and the rewards of our efforts will change from normal to exponential.

For a year and half, Ujjwal kept posting videos daily, and achieved a subscriber base of close to 400,000. But he was not making any money from YouTube advertisements because his account was in the validation stage. When he enquired about it, he was told there was a long queue for account verification, so even if his desired advertising revenue share had been allocated to him, he would receive it only after the verification was done. Ujjwal was surprised by this but he kept uploading the videos. He says, 'I was not creating videos to make money, so I didn't stop. However, I needed money to fund my ideas and buy paid games. So I looked to YouTube and after waiting a year, the money started coming in.'

Because of his 400,000 subscribers, Ujjwal was invited to a YouTube gamers' event. But no one recognised him there. On the other hand, people were taking selfies with YouTube gamers who had fewer subscribers. Returning home, Ujjwal shared his disappointment with Ankit. But Ankit pointed out that people did not know him because he never appeared in his videos. He suggested Ujjwal use a face-cam for his videos. Ujjwal had created over 300 videos along with commentary on the games he played. The use of commentary had brought him a newfound confidence. Now, considering Ankit's suggestion, he felt the time was right to use a face-cam in the videos.

From ancient times, humans have loved to tell and listen to stories. Movies and novels engage audiences through narratives carefully curated by their creators. These stories usually follow a linear structure, following the journey of the protagonist, and have a happy or sad ending. In contrast, interactive storytelling is a form in which the storyline is not planned. The choices of the audience shape it. In the case of video games, game players make decisions and judgements throughout the game, leading to numerous possibilities and tracks in the stories. Interestingly, with his unique style of interactive storytelling, Ujjwal has created a niche for himself in the crowded world of YouTube.

Ujjwal's strategy is to create a story that is very different from the game's original story. His *GTA* (*Grand Theft Auto*) series is very popular mainly because he created his own storyline in the game. He says, 'People are already aware of the original story. I use the same plot and characters with totally different storylines, and that creates excitement for people.' He does a desi commentary in all his videos, including cool desi dialogues. Whenever the story seems dry, he adds a little humour. His smiling face, warm personality and funny storytelling style have led to an exponential rise in subscribers. On 10 October 2020, he reached 9 million subscribers, which quickly increased to 10 million on 3 November 2020.

BE READY FOR FAILURES

When you are creating a new path for yourself, unexpected setbacks and challenges are par for the course. Before touching the rainbow's end, you have to go through many lows, failures and problems. But the reward belongs to those who believe in themselves and do not give up when setbacks arrive.

The South Korean company, PUBG Corporation, originally developed *PUBG* for PC and console. However, the mobile version of the game was launched and distributed by a Chinese tech company, Tencent. It is this connection that has put the game on the Indian government's radar. Before being banned in India, the *PUBG* tournament was the biggest virtual sports tournament in India, with crores of rupees in prize money. Ujjwal wanted to participate in the tournament, but could not practise with the low-end phone he had.

Seeing his brother's desire to participate in the *PUBG* tournament, Ankit bought an iPad for Ujjwal. But, by the time Ujjwal had become expert at playing the game on an iPad, the *PUBG* policies changed and using the iPad was no longer an option. Ankit sold the iPad and used the money to buy a good smartphone. He gave the smartphone to his mother to give Ujjwal after he was done with his studies. Meanwhile, Ujjwal's father met with an accident and was hospitalised. One night, Ujjwal's mother had to stay in the hospital, so she left the phone with Ujjwal. He kept playing the game till late at night and fell asleep without locking the front door. When he woke, the phone was gone. It had been stolen.

For the next two days, Ujjwal moped around dejected. His teachers in school were surprised to see the most talkative boy in class not uttering a word. Ujjwal's mother consoled him saying, 'Don't worry about the phone. We are happy that nothing happened to you.'

With whatever preparation he had done, Ujjwal entered the *PUBG* tournament, but lost in the semi-finals. Being a sportsperson, he knew winning and losing were parts of any game, that losing was temporary and he could make a comeback. Ujjwal says, 'I became very serious about the game. It was a single-minded focus where nothing else mattered. But I lost.'

To motivate Ujjwal, Ankit told him about Elon Musk, the founder of Tesla and SpaceX. Ujjwal watched many of Elon Musk's videos on YouTube and learnt how, before making Tesla and SpaceX highly successful companies, Elon had faced drastic failures. Ujjwal says, 'Like Steve Jobs, Elon Musk has also become a source of inspiration for me. He thinks at a different level and displays bold imagination and a high tolerance for risk.' Ujjwal also admires the deep research and study Elon Musk puts into his projects. Elon Musk's words, 'Failure is an option here. If things are not failing, you are not innovating enough,' motivates Ujjwal to try new things without getting disappointed by short-term failures.

By the time Ujjwal completed Class XII, he had come up with many ideas and wanted to work on them quickly. He told Ankit that he did not want to wait for three or four years to graduate before working on these ideas. Instead, he expressed his desire to join a coaching institute to learn programming languages, which would help him give shape to his ideas. Ankit discussed this with their parents and helped to create an option for Ujjwal. He received parental permission to delay joining a college for a year to focus on learning programming languages and game development.

Today, Ujjwal earns well from YouTube advertisements and brand deals. He has used these earnings to pay his coaching fee, buy a high-end smartphone and a world-class gaming set-up. He is also putting in effort and investing in gaming servers to promote *Minecraft* in India. *Minecraft* is considered to be one of the greatest video games of all time, but it is not very popular in India yet.

Ujjwal says, 'For parents worried about what their children are playing, this game helps to develop creativity and critical thinking.' Ujjwal's dream is to organise *Minecraft* tournaments in India on the lines of the *PUBG* tournaments. He says, 'I know I am taking a risk, but I will not stop trying just because of the risk, or fear of failure. Even if I fail, I will learn something invaluable.'

IN CONCLUSION

In his book *Outliers*, Malcolm Gladwell emphasises that in order to become world-class in any field, you need 10,000 hours of deliberate practice. Oscar-winning musician A.R. Rahman started playing piano at the age of four. Indian chess grandmaster Viswanathan Anand began playing chess when he was just six years old. The legendary Indian cricketer Sachin Tendulkar started playing cricket at the age of eleven. Imagine how many hours of practice must have gone into the success of these legends!

Because of his early start as a gaming YouTuber, Ujjwal has the benefit of practice time. However, he still has to reach 10,000 hours. He spends 14–15 hours a day playing games, developing games, promoting games and planning business opportunities around games. There is little doubt that his hunger, desire and determination will help him cross the 10,000 hours mark soon, and not only India, but the whole world will notice the rise of a gaming star.

Perspectives from Ujjwal Chaurasia

- If you want to become a YouTuber, or follow any other passion, then definitely go for it. But don't compromise on studies. Keep a balance.
- Only hard work will not take you far. Along with hard work you also need uniqueness.
- In today's age, you will find hundreds of enjoyable distractions. To achieve your dreams in the future, sacrifice your desire to enjoy in the present.
- Focus on gaining audience retention time. To start, create short 3–5-minute videos. If people watch these videos, even for a minute, then it means you are getting good audience retention. If your video is really good, then the audience will spend more time. I believe the more audience retention you get, the more YouTube promotes your video.
- Take care of your mental and physical health. If health suffers, then performance suffers, leading to poor video quality. If your video quality is poor, the audience will move on.

REFLECTIONS AND AFTERTHOUGHTS

The first version of this book was written in 2020–21. During the course of writing this book, we noticed that on the one hand, traditional entertainment sources such as Bollywood films and in-person were breaking under the strain of the COVID-19 pandemic, and on the other, the new entertainment sources, such as YouTube channels and video games were proliferating. The two years of the pandemic also saw an explosion in the popularity of stars, such as Pratik Gandhi (*Scam 1992*) and Pankaj Tripathi (*Mirzapur*), who were once regular actors in Bollywood, but became superstars on OTT.

While the pandemic was instrumental in driving traffic to the digital channels, their popularity and importance grew further after the pandemic when the world returned to normalcy. Indeed, the tide has shifted and we see room for further exponential growth. Here are some reasons for our confidence.

The popularity of India's top digital influencers is clear from the fact that many of them have more social media subscribers than venture capital funded start-ups, listed corporates and celebrity film stars. It is one reason why brands are relying more on digital celebrities. For instance, Ola Electric announced Bhuvan Bam as one of its celebrity brand ambassadors. Even traditional media is now taking digital influencers seriously. For example, *Business Today* featured CA Rachana Ranade on its cover. *Forbes India* started an annual list featuring 100 leading digital creators. The Government of India started National Creators Awards. Media channels like CNBC and MoneyControl have also covered influencers extensively. Creators are appearing in web series and movies and launching their merchandise brands.

We have also noticed another trend. As more founders recognise the potential of personal branding and content creation, a new category is emerging in the content creation realm as founders who have become influencers are now acknowledged as the latest breed of creators. While some founder-influencers captivate their audiences with tweets (Xs), others engage them through podcasts or video interviews. Examples include Anand Mahindra, the chairman of Mahindra and Mahindra; Harsh Goenka, the chairman of RPG; Harsh Mariwala, the chairman of Marico; and Nikhil and Nithin Kamath, founders of Zerodha, as well as the judges of Shark Tank. They mainly participate in educating audiences about start-ups and various aspects of entrepreneurship, creating content to reach a wider audience and build their own distribution.

Today, youngsters are being drawn to becoming content creators and social media influencers the way they were once attracted to becoming engineers, doctors and lawyers. One key reason for this rising interest is the financial windfall digital creators achieve, especially those with million-plus followers. While their videos are free to view, creators have multiple income streams, such as Google advertisements and brand collaborations. There are many creators in India making ₹10–15 lakhs a month. Clearly, these numbers attract people to become social media influencers rather than taking up a regular job.

We believe that the rise of the creator economy will surpass the most optimistic estimates in the coming years. The time is not far off when companies that made youngsters wait for hours for an interview will be waiting in line to sign brand and promotion deals with the same youngsters they had rejected in job interviews, but who are now popular on the internet. This scenario makes many a youngster optimistic about their future, which is good. But sometimes, optimism can cross the line and become arrogance, which is bad.

So, to keep ground realities in mind, we would like to highlight a few complexities. To hit lakhs in earnings, creators need millions of followers. And that is not easy. More than 500 hours of video is uploaded to YouTube every minute. So, the audience has an unlimited choice in entertainment. Also, to keep the audience coming back, creators have to post content regularly. The quality of the content is of supreme importance. It has to be informative, simple and unbiased. To add to the challenges of creators, presence on one platform is not sufficient. For instance, a YouTube video has to also be shared on other social media channels to gain traffic.

With constant algorithm changes on social media platforms, it's becoming increasingly difficult to determine the best way to reach your audience. Moreover, each platform has its own audience expectations. Between X (formerly Twitter), Instagram, YouTube and other platforms, creators have to cultivate different platform-centric personas and communities. Even within Instagram or YouTube alone, there's pressure to create various types of content—posts, videos, shorts and stories. Moreover, the audience is constantly evolving too, making it even tougher for content creators to predict what works and what doesn't.

It means a creator has to engage the audience on multiple tracks, which is super tough. The point we want to make here is that a tremendous amount of hard work goes on behind the scenes.

Social media usually portrays the positive aspects of people's lives, which psychologically impacts the way viewers perceive the life of creators. However, many creators who look happy are in fact filled with anxiety and stress because their video views are inconsistent.

Moreover, from the other side of the smartphone screen, it may look like everyone can become an influencer and monetise their content, but it's not easy for everyone to make a livable income off it. Even those who are successful in doing so claim that constant and steady income is unlikely or rare. According to a report by Kalaari Capital, there are around 80 million creators in India, of which only about 150,000 can monetise their services effectively—i.e., less than 0.2 per cent.

The Advertising Standards Council of India released guidelines for 'Influencer Advertising in Digital Media', to make viewers aware that a particular video contains promotional or paid content. Therefore, the content needs to be presented in a manner that is good for the audience, effective for the brand and credible for the creator. Checking all three boxes is again not easy and adds to the stress level of creators. To sustain their careers, creators need to also focus on their mental health.

By now, you will have understood something of both the opportunities and the challenges of the creator economy. Let us now share a middle ground that could help you stand out in the crowded and competitive digital world. The first wave of creators focused on English, followed by Hindi and Hinglish. But now, a huge opportunity exists in regional languages. As an example, Ankit Baiyanpuria is a wrestler-turned-fitness influencer with over 12 million followers on YouTube and Instagram, hails from Bayanpur, Sonipat, in Haryana. He always opens his workout videos with the phrase '*Ram Ram Bhai Sareya Ne*', which has endeared him to a lot of small-town youth. To cater to the demand of small towns, you can think of creating videos in regional languages, such as Marathi, Tamil, Malayalam and others.

Brands and audiences are not only looking for top creators but also emerging creators with their own domain niches. Over time, every niche, including comedy, beauty, fashion and lifestyle, business and finance, health and fitness, food, tech and travel, has become crowded. However, some creators are standing out by delving into more specific niches. For instance, Revant Himatsingka, popularly known as Food Pharmer, has carved out a unique identity by raising awareness about reading food labels on packaged foods.

We wish those creators who have made their mark all future success. At the same time, we look forward to the emergence of new creators. This book is not only a tribute to India's creator economy, but also a small contribution to its further growth. With the rise of more creators, the demand for their stories will also increase, so you can expect that we will be writing more volumes of these inspiring stories. We eagerly await the day when the creators we cover in our future books will tell us that this, our first book, played a meaningful role in their journeys.

But without our readers, we authors are nothing but leaves blowing in the wind. It is only with your support that we can achieve this dream.

ACKNOWLEDGEMENTS

This book would not have been possible without the advice, motivation and support of incredible people who contributed immensely to our endeavour. We have many people to thank!

Firstly, we would like to thank Pooja (Harsh's wife). She has always motivated him to achieve meaningful goals. When we started this book project, the world was not normal. COVID-19 had changed everything. Moreover, Yashvi (Harsh's daughter), was just eighteen months old. Along with her job, Pooja took care of everything at home so that Harsh could focus on this book, along with his professional commitments. Thank you, Pooja!

We would like to extend our heartfelt thanks to Viraj Sheth, co-founder and CEO of Monk Entertainment. When we began writing this book, Viraj listened to our idea and showed faith in it. Another person who supported our vision is Rohit Raj, co-founder and CEO of BB Ki Vines Productions. Thank you, Rohit, for your invaluable support! We also want to express our gratitude to Pranav Panpalia, founder of Opraahfx, for believing in our idea and being so helpful and supportive. They played a key role in connecting us with the creators covered in the book and finding time in their busy schedules.

We thank all the creators covered in this book. They gave us their valuable time and shared inputs with a lot of passion and patience. Thank you, Ashish Chanchlani! Thank you, Bhuvan Bam! Thank you, Ranveer Allahbadia! Thank you, Nikunj Lotia!

Thank you, Prajakta Koli! Thank you, Madan Gowri! Thank you, Yashraj Mukhate! Thank you, Ujjwal Chaurasia! Thank you, Kabita Singh! Thank you, Sonal Devraj and Nicole Concessao! Thank you, Abhi and Niyu!

A big thank you to Manish, Kabita Singh's husband, for sharing his valuable inputs on Kabita's story. A big thank you to Mohit and Dharmesh at Opraahfx, for their support in covering Ujjwal Chaurasia's journey. And a big thank you to Sourav at One Digital Entertainment, for his support in closing Prajakta Koli's story.

We are grateful to Nishant Sengupta, a first-year student of mass media at Ramnarain Ruia College, Mumbai, for his invaluable help in reviewing our write-ups. His feedback on the early drafts helped us a lot in improving the stories.

To add more credibility to our book, we needed testimonials from some renowned people. Fortunately, Anand Kumar, who runs the famous Super 30 programme (yes, Hrithik Roshan's movie *Super 30* is a biopic on the life of Anand Sir), agreed to bless our book with his testimonial. As luck would have it, Dr Sandeep Goyal, a renowned ad man, who heads Rediffusion, one of India's oldest and biggest ad agencies, also blessed our book with his testimonial. When we approached bestselling author Dr Radhakrishnan Pillai, chiefly famous for spreading Chanakya's teachings in the modern world, we received a lot of encouragement. He was glad to know about our book and blessed it with his testimonial. By good luck, we also received blessings and a testimonial from famous Wharton professor Kartik Hosanagar, recognised as one of the world's top 40 business professors under 40. We are thankful to Arunabh Kumar, the founder of TVF and the man behind *Pitchers*, *Aspirants*, *Panchayat*, *Kota Factory* and many other famous web series, for his blessings and testimonial.

Special thanks to Aurodeep Mukherjee, Commissioning Editor at Westland Books. He gave us a patient hearing and helped in the book's selection for publication by Westland. He also helped in making the book much better. Thank you, Aurodeep, we are so lucky to have had a chance to work with you. We are also thankful to Gautam Padmanabhan and Karthika V.K. at Westland Books for their tremendous support. We thank Saurabh Garge for giving our book the beauty it deserves. We are incredibly grateful to every team member at Westland. We are thankful to Swarup Nanda, Preeti Chib, Malini Nair, Chandralekha Maitra, Ashish Samant, Priyanka Sawant, Sunny Agarwal, Kavita Singh and the entire team at Pencil and Leadstart for their support in publishing the first edition of this book.

Special thanks to Prashant Sinha and his team at Prashant Arts, for creating the beautiful caricatures for the book. Thank you, Prashant, for your valuable support!

We want to acknowledge Prakash Iyer's books *The Habit of Winning* (Penguin, 2011) and *The Secret of Leadership* (Penguin, 2013) and Shiv Khera's book *You Can Win* (Macmillan, 1998) for some of the anecdotes and parables used in this book.

Finally, we would like to thank everyone who has helped us in shaping our journey.